EMBEDDED BUSINESS
LIBRARIANSHIP
FOR THE
PUBLIC LIBRARIAN

EMBEDDED BUSINESS LIBRARIANSHIP FOR THE PUBLIC LIBRARIAN

BARBARA A. ALVAREZ

AN IMPRINT OF THE AMERICAN LIBRARY ASSOCIATION

CHICAGO 2016

BARBARA A. ALVAREZ has been teaching and training the public for five years. As a librarian, Alvarez has partnered with local government, historical centers, nonprofit groups, and the business community. When she served as the business liaison librarian for nearly two years at the Barrington Area Library in Barrington, Illinois, she taught over 150 job seekers, completed more than 100 one-on-one appointments with local business owners and professionals, and coproduced numerous videos and podcasts with entrepreneurs. For her efforts, Alvarez was nominated for the Athena Leadership Award for innovation and creativity in the business community, and was awarded the Public Librarian Support Award from the Business Reference and Services Section (BRASS)/Morningstar at the 2015 American Library Association conference. Alvarez has presented at professional networking events on the topic of business librarianship and has been a contributor to *Public Libraries Online,* as well as being published in *Library Journal, Illinois Libraries Matter,* and Recruiter.com.

© 2016 by the American Library Association

Extensive effort has gone into ensuring the reliability of the information in this book; however, the publisher makes no warranty, express or implied, with respect to the material contained herein.

ISBNs
978-0-8389-1474-8 (paper)
978-0-8389-1481-6 (PDF)
978-0-8389-1482-3 (ePub)
978-0-8389-1483-0 (Kindle)

Library of Congress Cataloging-in-Publication Data

Names: Alvarez, Barbara, 1989– author.
Title: Embedded business librarianship for the public librarian / Barbara Alvarez.
Description: Chicago : ALA Editions, an imprint of the American Library Association, 2016. | Includes bibliographical references and index.
Identifiers: LCCN 2016021770| ISBN 9780838914748 (pbk. : alk. paper) | ISBN 9780838914816 (pdf : alk. paper) | ISBN 9780838914823 (epub : alk. paper) | ISBN 9780838914830 (kindle : alk. paper)
Subjects: LCSH: Libraries and business—United States. | Libraries and industry—United States. | Public librarians—Professional relationships. | Business librarians—Professional relationships.
Classification: LCC Z711.75 A48 2016 | DDC 027.6/9—dc23
LC record available at https://lccn.loc.gov/2016021770

Cover design by Alejandra Diaz. Images © Rawpixel/Shutterstock, Inc. Text design in the Chaparral, Gotham, and Bell Gothic typefaces. Composition by Dianne M. Rooney.

♾ This paper meets the requirements of ANSI/NISO Z39.48-1992 (Permanence of Paper).

Printed in the United States of America

20 19 18 17 16   5 4 3 2 1

For Nick

Contents

Acknowledgments

I WOULD LIKE TO EXPRESS MY SINCERE GRATITUDE TO the Barrington Area Library, particularly Detlev Pansch and Rose Faber, for their constant support and encouragement in my role as the embedded business librarian. Additionally, I would like to thank the business librarians that I have been so fortunate to connect with during my time as embedded business librarian, particularly those in the northwest Chicago suburbs and Library Biz Connect in Michigan.

I would also like to thank Jamie Santoro, editor at ALA Editions, for her support and guidance throughout the writing and publication of this book.

Introduction

LIBRARY PROFESSIONALS OFTEN FALL INTO POSITIONS, roles, or library practices that we did not foresee. After all, the nature of public libraries is to adapt our library collections, functions, and priorities to the needs of our community. That being said, we all need support and guidance—that is where this book comes in. *Embedded Business Librarianship for the Public Librarian* was written to introduce those who are completely new to this type of librarianship to the mission, purpose, and practice of embedded business librarianship in public libraries.

The first chapter introduces you to "Embedded Business Librarianship," as well as understanding the distinction between outreach and embedded librarianship. Embedded business librarianship means that a librarian leaves the physical library space and becomes integrated within the business community and its dialogue. An embedded business librarian not only cultivates awareness of the library's resources and expertise, but also is a valued contributor to the business community's conversation.

Before becoming embedded in the business community, it is imperative to understand the scope of the business landscape. The second chapter will describe the recommended research to conduct, including major industries, business size and expenditures, and emerging trends to understand the breadth of the business community. This will allow you to develop an idea of the needs, goals, and opportunities in your public library's business community.

After doing background research about the business community, it can often be confusing and intimidating for librarians to make initial steps to reach out to these organizations, businesses, and professionals. A five-step process will be outlined in the third chapter. This will provide you with the action plan that you need to become embedded in the business community.

Small business owners, professionals, and job seekers are the main groups of the library's business community. It is important for the embedded business librarian to understand the goals of each unique group, as well as to learn the best way to approach and engage them. Finally, the fourth chapter will offer recommendations for forming sustainable partnerships with each group.

In addition to networking in the community, the embedded business librarian will design and deliver engaging, educational, and informative opportunities that will bring the business community inside the library. Additionally, creating a coworking environment is vital for business community collaboration. Suggestions for how to proceed will be described in the fifth chapter.

The embedded business librarian role often requires that the librarian become a liaison between the public library and business and career organizations in the community. The purpose of the liaison role is to ensure proper communication between the library and its patrons and the business community. An outline of potential organizations to partner with, as well as an overview of incorporating the liaison part of the embedded business librarian role, will be outlined in the sixth chapter.

Sometimes librarians shy away from working with the business community because they may not have a business background or a support network with fellow librarians. A focus on recommended books, blogs, news sources, online training, and joining or forming a librarian support group will be detailed in the seventh chapter.

In the eighth and final chapter, we will connect all of the elements of becoming an embedded business librarian and building transformative connections in your library's business community. When we combine these elements together, you can see the true value and impact of this role.

1
Embedded Business Librarianship

- The essentials of embedded business librarianship, including its goal, why it's important to your library and community, and how it differs from providing outreach

- How embedded business librarianship impacts community-business relationships

- The best way to use this book for developing your embedded business librarianship role

Are you the business librarian at your public library or do you happen to be the one that everybody in your department refers to when they need help with business research? Are you a librarian who promotes the library within the community at events or other functions? Maybe you are a manager who realizes that your library needs to improve its relationships with the local community, specifically the business community. Perhaps you fill none of these roles, but you want to build strong connections with local business owners, professionals, and job seekers. Whatever the case may be, welcome to *Embedded Business Librarianship for the Public Librarian.*

For some, this may seem scary and for others exciting. There may be some readers who are uncertain, while others cannot wait to get started. Whatever you are feeling at this point, we will walk through the entire process of becoming an embedded business librarian together. Throughout this book, we will discuss the ideology and process of becoming integrated in the local business community, as well as the importance of building relationships that will transform your library's relationship with the members of your local business community. By the time you have finished reading this book, you will have a fresh perspective on what it means to be truly embedded with the local business community, as well as the role that you and your public library will have for sustaining meaningful relationships with that community. So, let's get started.

EMBEDDED BUSINESS LIBRARIAN

First things first: what exactly is an embedded business librarian? Whether you use the title "Embedded Business Librarian" or some other job description is immaterial; the philosophy and ideology of this role are what matter the most. An embedded business librarian is a library professional who is rooted in his or her public library's business community. To be rooted in the public library's business community means that this role will become *part* of the business community instead of remaining separated from it. An embedded business librarian strives to be an equal partner in the business community and have an equal voice. Small business owners, professionals, and job seekers see the embedded business librarian as a peer, colleague, and fellow business community member instead of an outsider who solely represents the library.

The ultimate goal of the embedded business librarian is to become integrated in the business community as much as possible, and not be viewed strictly as "the library" or "the librarian." This attitude and relationship will guide how you function in this position and will affect the activities that you participate in, the committees that you join, the projects that you work on, and the way that you and others see librarians and the library. Ultimately, this will impact the role and services that the library provides to the business community.

OUTREACH VS. EMBEDDED LIBRARIANSHIP

Being an embedded business librarian is significantly different than outreach. Everybody defines outreach differently, but often outreach can be thought of as a library professional stepping away from the reference desk and into the community as needed. Sometimes this means setting up a booth at a local farmer's market, or doing a presentation at the high school before the summer reading club begins, or speaking to the town or village about a library initiative, like "foods for fines." In each of these instances, the purpose is typically to remind or inform people about their local library and to *promote* the library. This is perhaps the greatest difference between embedded librarianship and performing outreach.

To begin with, embedded business librarianship is not necessarily about promoting the library, although the library is certainly promoted within the process. Instead, embedded business librarianship means that you are part of the business community's conversation, not separated from it, so this could entail leaving the library and going into the business community several times per week. Embedded business librarianship means that instead of going to community functions to give sound bites about the library and why people should support the library, or presuming to know how the library can support them, you will be attending meetings, joining committees, and networking in ways that emphasize the library's desire to learn and understand the business community as a peer. This will certainly be a mental shift for many libraries and will probably involve a conversation with library management about the functions and expectations of this role.

Both outreach and embedded librarianship are laudable efforts for public libraries. Indeed, any time the public library makes efforts outside its own walls is a success. Depending on the staff size of your library, outreach may seem more accessible than an embedded business librarian role. However, you can certainly implement embedded philosophy into an outreach model. The core concept is to make a concerted effort to be genuinely integrated in the business community.

THE CASE FOR EMBEDDED BUSINESS LIBRARIANSHIP

For those of you who are uncertain, you may be wondering why we even *need* public librarians to be embedded in the business community. After all, shouldn't the business owners, professionals, and job seekers be coming into the library—not the reverse? You may be wondering, "Do we have enough staff to properly cover the desk in addition to sending them out into the community?" Make no mistake: embedded business librarianship is an important role for the public library.

According to the Small Business Association's Office of Advocacy, there are 27.9 million small business owners that accounted for 64 percent of "the net new jobs created between 1993 and 2011."[1] Furthermore, there are nearly 18 million independent workers, or "solopreneurs," and this growing number shows no sign of slowing.[2] Additionally, the Great Recession proved to library critics that libraries are needed more than ever—just ask the 36 percent of patrons who used the library in 2012 for job search assistance.[3] Although this number has gone down to 23 percent (which is a good thing), there is still strong support for the public library to provide business resources and workshops. In fact, 52 percent "of all Americans 16 and older say libraries should 'definitely' create programs for local businesses and entrepreneurs."[4] Clearly there is data that expresses the need of the national business community for library services.

So, what does this mean? Since some job seekers already come to the library, does that mean that we do not need to reach out to them?

Since there is a clear interest in business workshops at the library, should we just send out a few friendly e-mails to local business owners and hope that they'll stop by? Should our library create some programs, promote them on social media and in the library newsletter, and feel that we did enough? Hardly.

In fact, what the data given above means is that it is the perfect climate to go outside the library and into the community and meet the business owners, professionals, and job seekers where they are and build relationships with them. It is important not to seize this moment as just an opportunity to boost program attendance and door count numbers, but instead to put energy into forming and sustaining meaningful connections. The data above is just a small fraction of evidence that shows how receptive the business community can be to the library becoming a part of the lives of business owners, professionals, and job seekers.

Take a moment to consider how much of your library's community is impacted by job growth, small business success, and employment. When a small business owner is making progress with help from the library, when a professional receives the information that they need from the library for an important company presentation, and when a job seeker learns from the library how to tailor their job search, their own well-being, as well as the well-being of their friends, family, colleagues, neighbors, and surroundings are greatly impacted. Moreover, the feeling of genuine support and championship that the business community has because of the library's embedded involvement could just be the push they need to move forward with a new initiative or project. In essence, when the public library invests in building relationships with the business community, it is investing in the livelihood, well-being, and future of all of its citizens. As public library professionals, this should not be optional, but a core mission for us.

While statistics may point to the value of libraries among small business owners, professionals, and job seekers, this certainly does not capture the entirety of the business community's relationship with the public library. There are still plenty of people who view their local public library as outdated and obsolete. On the other hand, there is often great reverence for the library because people respect what the library represents: education, literacy, and opportunity. Yet many people do not really know *how* the library could fit into their lives, particularly their professional lives.

When members of the business community are informed of the resources, workshops, technology, or other ongoing engagement projects at the library, they are often amazed and intrigued, and are prompted to learn more. This appreciation becomes greater when librarians develop meaningful relationships and work with business-people on committees and socialize with them in networking groups. In essence, this appreciation can turn to mutual advocacy.

No longer does the library have to tout its own accomplishments and worthiness, because now other people can do that for the library. Anyone knows how much more valuable it is to have peers vouch for an organization than it is to have the organization vouch for itself. To use a business analogy, people often tell job seekers that when they are networking they should not necessarily be asking others for interviews and job leads, but rather should ask others how *they* can be of service *to them*. In turn, when someone does learn of a job opening or promotional opportunity, they are happy to return the favor to the job seeker who has already been of service to them. This holds true for how the library will integrate itself into the business community: we will demonstrate how the library is relevant to the business community by supporting its members, who in turn will support and understand the library on a deeper level.

THE MAIN GOAL OF EMBEDDED BUSINESS LIBRARIANSHIP

Every community and library has specific goals for how they want to improve connections with their business community. And through the embedded business model, relationships will indeed change and new opportunities will be created or discovered. That being said, the overall goal for this position is a consistent focus on learning and understanding the business community on a meaningful level, as well as positioning the library as an organization that is part of the business community. As library professionals, we tend to assume that because *we* view the library as relevant and an integral part of the community, that others must also. But the truth is, many people view the library as irrelevant.

However, embedded business librarianship is not self-serving. It comes from a true and honest attempt to really understand, learn, and be an equal partner with the business community. This means stepping back and listening—not just telling the business community what you think they want or should hear. It also means demonstrating the library's care for the business community, not just saying it. Embedded business librarianship recognizes that you do not know or have to know all the answers to the issues or struggles that the business community may face, because you are going to work with them toward a solution, not try to *be* the solution.

As you increase your interactions and engagement with the business community, you will undoubtedly discover that they very well may be the same people who serve on local charitable committees and school boards and local government. You may find that you already see them in the library, but as community members, not as business members. Essentially, when you develop relationships with the business community, you are developing relationships with the entire community.

GETTING STARTED

Before getting started, it is time to have a clear conversation with the management team at your library about the expectations for this role. If you come from a library that expects deliverables from every event, workshop, demonstration, or speaking engagement, this will be an especially important discussion. Support from colleagues and management is crucial, especially during the beginning when so much of this is experimental, and you need to see where your library fits into the equation.

When you are embedded in the business community, your outcomes will not always be consistent, especially in the beginning. You may attend functions where you feel that you did not make an impact or you did not make a connection, and your library needs to support your role with an understanding that it is not intended to boost programming statistics, reference questions, or door counts. While it is true that this will happen *in time*, many marks of success are going to be aspects that you cannot put onto paper but you will notice regardless. An example of an improvement that you cannot necessarily quantify is when you go to events or committees in the community and people start referring you to others and speaking positively about your role or the library's opportunities.

That being said, depending on your library's management and board philosophy, you may need to come up with ways to quantify this new role without impeding its progress. Some examples:

- How many events did you attend monthly?
- If you speak at an event, how many people have you reached?
- Report news, trends, and data that you are learning in this new role and how these relate to the larger community and the library.

If you need to speak to the board about this new role, an emphasis on what you are learning and the relationships that you are developing can complement any of the above statistics.

Another mistaken belief is that you may feel you need to be a business expert to get started in this role. That is not true. While it can certainly be helpful to have a business background, an interest, curiosity, and desire to learn more about business are the most important assets of the role. We will discuss how to boost your business knowledge through continuing education in a later chapter, but rest assured that the most important aspect is your knowledge of your library and your own eagerness and desire to make a difference. If a library professional possesses these qualities, there is no reason that he or she cannot be an embedded business librarian.

HOW RELATIONSHIPS WILL TRANSFORM

Depending on how often your library has already positioned itself in the community, you may be treading on brand-new territory. Regardless if you already have a solid business relationship foundation or your library is a complete novice, you will no doubt feel awkward and out of place in the beginning of this role. There may be times where you will feel tongue-tied, confused, or just simply like you do not belong. However, you will absolutely develop confidence and a sense of who you are and how the library fits into the conversation with business members.

In moments of doubt, it helps to reflect on the reason why you are the embedded business librarian. When you focus on building relationships from a genuine belief that you want what is best for your library's community and you want to add value to people's lives, it keeps you driven, focused, and motivated, particularly during the beginning period when you are still trying to adapt.

As you continue in the embedded business librarian role, you will go from an outsider who has to be clued into the goings-on in the community to one who is aware of the latest developments, trends, and events. Instead of hosting a table at the community event, you may be on the committee for organizing the event; instead of attending a business "Lunch and Learn," you may be invited to speak at the lunch. Instead of going to a local speaking engagement, you may have been one of the people to help select the speaker. Instead of introducing yourself at village merchant meetings, you will be able to update everyone on trends at the library and stay abreast of trends in the community. You will also learn how the library can host ongoing projects, events, and platforms that directly serve the business community.

The bottom line is that you can expect relationships with the business community to transform from transactional to interactional.

Q & A

How should I use this book as a guide?

This book was written with the purpose of introducing people who are new to this type of librarianship to the core tenets and practices of being embedded in the business community. It will discuss how you can do preliminary research, make connections with the business community, and build upon those connections in ways that will make the library an integral organization to the business community in ways that are realistic and sustainable.

The book has detailed step-by-step instructions, as well as recommended practices for increasing engagement and developing courses and programs for your business community. The chapters are comprehensive and the more you try, the more confident and directed you will feel.

Keep in mind that this is a learning process and there will be many trial-and-error experiences that come along with this role. Once you have positioned yourself in the business community, you will be able to make the role into one that is unique and specific to your library and its community.

DON'T BE AFRAID TO GET STARTED!

You might feel pressured to do everything at once, so don't be afraid to start small. Recognize that this is a process and will take time. Even if you feel that you are not making progress, you have not failed—and will not fail—because you are serving your community to the best of your ability. So have patience with yourself and with the community. Encourage yourself to learn new technology, trends, relationship interactions, and everything else that comes with your role.

FINAL THOUGHTS

The embedded business librarian's main objective is to become an equal partner and colleague with members of the business community.

This means that you will not be seen as an outsider who occasionally comes into the business community to promote the library's services. Instead, you will become a consistent voice and peer. As we go through this book, we will discuss methods by which you can put this philosophy into practice. In the beginning, it may feel more like outreach, but that can be a natural progression to becoming embedded. We will also discuss how you can organize the library's services and programs to reflect the relationships that you build in the business community. When you have relationships with business owners, professionals, and job seekers based on a genuine desire to work together, your entire role and the practices of the library will be impacted.

LET'S SUM IT UP

- Embedded business librarianship is about becoming an equal voice and partner in your library's business community.

- Being embedded is different than outreach because you will be developing long-lasting relationships.

- When the library cares about the economic growth of its community, it shows that it cares about its citizens and their livelihoods.

- The ultimate goal of embedded business librarianship is a consistent focus on learning and understanding the business community on a meaningful level, as well as positioning the library as an organization that is part of the business community.

- Discuss with your management team new ways to track your success and the outcomes in this role.

- Relationships will transform from transactional to interactional.

- Use this book as a guide to getting started, but don't be afraid to make adjustments or try new initiatives according to your library and community needs.

NOTES

1. "SBA Office of Advocacy: Frequently Asked Questions," Small Business Association Office of Advocacy, September 1, 2012, https://www.sba.gov/sites/default/files/FAQ_Sept_2012.pdf.

2. "The State of Independence in America: Third Annual Workforce Report," MBO Partners, September 1, 2013, http://info.mbopartners.com/rs/mbo/images/2013-MBO_Partners_State_of_Independence_Report.pdf.

3. John B. Horrigan, "Libraries at the Crossroads," Pew Research Center Internet Science Tech RSS, Pew Research Center, September 15, 2015, www.pewinternet.org/2015/09/15/libraries-at-the-crossroads.

4. Ibid.

2

Getting to Know Your Library's Business Community

IN THIS CHAPTER, WE WILL LEARN

- The importance of researching major industries, businesses, and trends to better understand the local business community landscape

- Why this data can help you prepare for connecting with local businesses and organizations

- How to conduct an informational interview for more details about the business community

Now that you have an understanding of the essentials of embedded business librarianship and what it means to be embedded in your library's business community, let's talk about what you need to do to take on this exciting new endeavor. In this chapter, we will focus on laying the groundwork for getting to know more about your public library's business community so that you can start building transformational relationships.

We will go over the behind-the-scenes practices that you can do to get yourself equipped with the information, resources, and knowledge that you need to make a solid first impression and lasting impact in your library's business community. For this chapter, we will only be going outside the library very briefly for an informational interview.

As we go through the different steps in this chapter, think of this exercise as if you were looking from a bird's-eye view and then zooming into each section for more details. This analogy will help you bring together the different puzzle pieces of the business community.

MAJOR INDUSTRIES

The first question to ask yourself is pretty obvious: what are the major industries in my library's business community?

You may be able to answer this question without doing any research at all, especially if your town is specifically known for a certain company, product, or service. For other people completing this exercise, the answer may not be so apparent. Regardless of what you think your business community's industries are, perform the exercise and you will probably be surprised at what the top results will be.

To get started on this research, take a look at these helpful resources:

- United States Census: American Fact Finder. Search by community and from there search within various topics, including Business and Industry. Within that category, you can search for Industry and Occupation Earnings, as well as Economy-Wide Key Statistics (http://factfinder .census.gov/faces/nav/jsf/pages/index.xhtml).
- County Business Patterns: This tool allows you to research on small-scale economy and markets (www.census.gov/ econ/cbp).

- Reference USA and A to Z Databases are paid subscriptions that allow you to select your area and search by major industry trends (www.referenceusa.com/Home/Home) and (www.atozdatabases.com/home).
- Hoover's Database is another paid subscription for in-depth company and industry reports (www.hoovers.com).
- Reach out to the local Chamber of Commerce for their statistics.

When you are looking over this data, consider these questions:

- How long has this industry been in your community?
- Is this a new trend or is it something that the community has been known for?
- What are the second and third most popular industries? How do they impact the first industry? Do they work together or are they in direct competition with one another?
- What are the industries that are not so popular but are gaining ground? How can they be supported by the library?
- Do people who work in these industries live locally or do they commute from other areas?

This will help you start thinking of and viewing your community from a different perspective. In the past, you may have looked at your library's community as a nameless, nondescript group of constituents to which you provide information services. Now you can start to see them in a new way that will impact how you evolve as an embedded librarian, as well as how you can tailor library services to them.

Once you have looked at your community's industry on a smaller scale, take a look at the industry landscape on a broader scale. This means looking at state, national, and international industry trends. Some of this information you can find on library subscription databases and others you can find online. Here are some suggested resources:

- Morningstar Research Investment Center is a paid sub-scription that has industry reports (www.morningstar .com/).

- EBSCO Regional Business News (https://www.ebscohost .com/academic/regional-business-news) and Business Searching Interface (http://support.ebsco.com/ knowledge_base/detail.php?id=2145) are other paid subscriptions for in-depth business tools and research.

- *The Economist*'s Special Reports (www.eiu.com/landing/ special_reports) provide access to data from various countries.

- U.S. Department of Commerce's Bureau of Economic Analysis (http://bea.gov/) provides briefings on different industry sections on a regional, national, and international scale.

As you look at the industry landscape on a broader scale, consider these questions:

- How does this compare to your local industry?

- What are the industry's SWOT analysis (Strengths, Weakness, Opportunities, and Threats)?

- What do you foresee are the changes that could happen in this industry in the next year, five years, and ten years?

- How will this impact the library's relationship with the businesses in this industry?

Some of the industry landscapes may surprise you while others may seem obvious. Regardless, this exercise will help you understand

For in-depth business resources, Celia Ross's *Making Sense of Business Reference: A Guide for Librarians and Information Professionals* (Chicago: ALA Editions, 2013) will guide you to valuable resources and help you gain confidence in conducting business research.

your library's business community and the industries within it in a new way.

BUSINESSES, BUSINESS SIZE, AND EXPENDITURES

Now that we have concentrated on the industry landscape locally, nationally, and internationally, let's zoom in and focus more on businesses. *How many businesses are in your library's business community?* The resources listed above, as well as in Celia Ross's book, can help you answer the following questions:

- How many businesses fit into the top five industries that you researched?
- How new are these businesses? Have they been around for a while or are they new additions to the area?

Take this information and continue to zoom in with the following questions:

- How big are these businesses in terms of employees? What is their average size?
- How much are businesses spending each month?
- Are they stand-alone businesses or do they have branches and other locations?
- How many are home-based?

Depending on the information that you uncover, you may find some details that are significantly more important to you than others. This can greatly impact how you plan to operate as an embedded business librarian. For example, if you learn that your library's business community consists of 80 percent of businesses with less than five employees or are significantly home-based, you can determine that these businesses possibly are family-owned and run by entrepreneurs who may be hoping to expand their business. Subsequently, you can adjust library business initiatives and resources to meet these entrepreneurial patrons.

EMERGING TRENDS

We have done quite a bit of research so far by studying your community's industry on a national and local level, the types of businesses and industries that dominate your community, and how this will impact these businesses' relationships with the library. The next step in this process is going to be discovering what the emerging trends are in your library's business community and the trends on a national and international scale.

Knowing emerging trends is very important because this can help you become more confident in your business and industry knowledge, but it also allows you to truly understand what the business owners and professionals in your business community are going through at this moment and what future business changes they are anticipating.

For example, let's take a look at how smartphones have revolutionized business and how this can be an example of how your business community is impacted by emerging trends. Cell phones impacted how quickly people could get in contact with other people, businesses, and stores. At the same time, the Internet improved the ability to find the information that they need. However, smartphones took these two landscapes and put them together in the form of Internet navigability and apps. How has that impacted the hospitality and transportation industries? Tremendously. No longer do people have to stay at hotels or motels or take taxis or limos. With app-based companies like Uber and Airbnb, people have the flexibility to find locations and prices that fit their needs at the push of a few buttons, and from any location.

For this reason, it is critical to stay abreast with emerging trends, particularly in the business and technology world, since they will likely dictate how your business community will transform in the future. Studying these trends does not mean that you need to read the *Wall Street Journal* every day. What is most important is that you are consistently reading and getting alerts on related trends. Here are two easy ways to stay in the know:

- Personalize your Google News with general business and technology topics, as well as specific companies, like Apple, Google, and Facebook, that set trends across industries.

- Set up a list on Twitter that follows major companies or news outlets, and regularly search under trending topics related to business, technology, or fields in your business community.

For research specifically on the job seekers in your area, take a look at these resources:

- Access the American Fact Finder and look at unemployment rates in your community (http://factfinder.census .gov/faces/nav/jsf/pages/index.xhtml).

- United States Department of Labor: Bureau of Labor Statistics gives you data on a national, state, and county level, as well as job turnover rates and employment projections (www.bls.gov/).

- U.S. Small Business Administration (SBA): Employment Statistics (https://www.sba.gov/content/employment -statistics) provides a generous list of resources for researching wage data, labor force statistics, women in the workforce, and equal opportunity employment statistics.

INFORMATIONAL INTERVIEWS

As mentioned previously, we will be developing a master plan for reaching out to your library's business community and forming your

Q & A

I understand how to gather information about business owners and industries, but what about the job seekers? How is this information relevant and how can it be beneficial for them?

The information that you are gathering in this section directly relates to the job seekers in your area for many reasons:

- The more you know about your library's business community, the more you will be aware of local opportunities and resources to which you can direct job seekers.

- The more you know about industry trends and how they impact your library's business community, the more you can develop courses and offer information to job seekers that will help them stay knowledgeable and competitive.

- Job seekers can be interested in starting a side business until they find something more permanent or are interested in becoming entrepreneurs as a career transition. The information that you gather will help them come up with business plans and topics that will give them more leverage.

In essence, the better informed you are about the business community on a local and national level, the greater your ability to help everybody who is impacted by the business community: business owners, professionals, and job seekers.

role as an embedded librarian. Before we reach out to the business community, conducting an informational interview can give you a bit more insight.

Set up an appointment with the director of the Chamber of Commerce, the Village Hall administration, and any local career centers. Additionally, if the library already partners with a local business owner or hosts some job-seeker workshops, see if there is anyone from these avenues that you can talk to for a brief informational interview.

Suggestions for Setting Up an Informational Interview

If you have been nervous about stepping into this new role, especially if you have not previously done much work outside the library building, this is a great opportunity to ease your way into the business community without taking on too much responsibility or commitment.

Because time is sensitive, send a brief e-mail asking for an appointment to chat for about 15–20 minutes about trends in the business and job-seeking arena. Explain that you are hoping to tailor library interactions with the community to meet the needs of local business owners, job seekers, and professionals and that you would appreciate the opportunity to learn more from their perspective.

In your meeting, consider asking some of these questions:

- What is your favorite part of the business community?
- What do you see business owners and entrepreneurs really passionate about?
- What do you think they struggle with the most?
- How has the business landscape for business owners or job seekers changed in the last five years?
- Have you noticed any recent significant changes that will impact the business community or job-seeker networking groups?

Obviously, you will have specific questions and conversation points based on the background research that you have conducted regarding industry types, business size and expenditures, and emerging trends. You may even walk away from this conversation with some advice on how you can go forward with your next steps or which partner organizations or businesses you can reach out to.

The purpose of these interviews is not to uncover all of the strengths and opportunities in your library's business community; that is something that can only be accomplished in the embedded librarian role when you have gained the confidence of job seekers, professionals, and business owners. Rather, the purpose of these informational interviews is to get another perspective on the information that you have been researching and gathering. The responses and feedback that you acquire in this section will be useful for you when you are stepping into your role as an embedded business librarian.

FINAL THOUGHTS

We accomplished quite a bit in the second chapter. Initially, we went over the value of doing background research before reaching out to members of the business community, and we acquired an understanding of the value of business and industry statistics. We also discussed the value of studying emerging trends and getting some additional information from local directors or business owners in your community. Additionally, we learned how this information will not only make you more knowledgeable about your library's business community, but also help you understand how the economy and overall industry trends impact their trade. Furthermore, we now understand how this connects to the job seekers in your library's community and how they can also benefit from your knowledge of the business community on a local and national level.

With all of this information at hand, you are ready to move onto the next step where you are actually going to go out into the community and start establishing yourself as an embedded business librarian.

LET'S SUM IT UP

- By looking at industries, you gain an overview with the broadest scope of the business landscape in your library's business community.

- When you learn more details about local business sizes and expenditures, you can start to consider how this impacts the local economy and where the library fits in.

- The information that you gather about local businesses and entrepreneurs will be just as useful for helping job seekers navigate their career transitions.

- Informational interviews can give you some primary insight into the business landscape and help direct your efforts into mapping out your next steps.

3

Navigating the Business Community

IN THIS CHAPTER, WE WILL LEARN

- How to create your networking list

- The best way to reach out to your contacts

- How to make a positive, lasting impression

- The importance of creating a follow-up opportunity

- The best steps for continued networking

You are now ready to start building lasting, transformative relationships with business owners, professionals, and job seekers. This step in the process is perhaps the most critical part of becoming embedded and taking your library's business services to the next level. These suggestions for becoming embedded in your business community are what separate libraries that simply offer business services and resources from libraries that are engaged, connected, and equal partners. Don't worry if you feel nervous or uncertain—we'll navigate the business community together.

FIVE STEPS TO EMBEDDED BUSINESS LIBRARIANSHIP

Below are the five steps to creating effective connections with your local business community and the framework for positioning yourself as the embedded business librarian. When you complete all five of these steps, you will not be embedded, but you will be well on your way toward becoming embedded in the community. This guide is simply the pathway toward going from outsider to equal partner. The exciting aspect is that it is an evergreen plan: you will be able to implement and adapt this to countless situations, organizations, and business groups.

Before you get started, remember the guiding principle of being embedded: *the public library adds value to the business community*. You may have to remind yourself that you are not to judge situations, predetermine needs, or be a superhero who can solve all business problems. Indeed, you may not know the answers or have solutions to certain scenarios that are presented to you; you need to remind yourself that this is okay. You are entering the business community **to** *build meaningful relationships* by learning about businesses' needs, opportunities, strengths, and aspirations.

STEP 1

Create a Networking List

From the initial research that you have already completed, you probably have an idea of the types of businesses and organizations that would partner the best with the library. Additionally, you may have even made some connections at events that you have attended in the past. Now is the time to draw up a document where you can create an action plan for the businesses, groups, individuals, and organizations with which you would like to initially build connections. The goal of this action plan is to list the names of businesses, networking groups, organizations, or professionals and a proposed way that you can reach out to them. You still may not know much about them, but you'll learn more about your business community as you build stronger connections with them. This will be a valuable opportunity to introduce yourself and start forming a working relationship.

Below is a list of organizations that you may want to consider when creating your list. As mentioned before, you will also want to include small businesses and individuals. These, of course, will be unique to your community.

- Chamber of Commerce
- Career centers
- Small business development center
- Networking committees
- Village Hall administration, specifically a merchant group or economic group
- Community colleges' job-seeker groups
- Professional networking groups
- SCORE Association (www.score.org)
- Rotary Club or other fraternal organizations
- Shopping centers: sometimes they have merchant gatherings for stores in the center
- Church employment centers
- Meetup.com: this is a great way to find out about local entrepreneurs, interests, and business groups. Additionally, you can create your own meetup group.
- Entrepreneur forums

Obviously, this is a general list. Depending on your community, you may have completely similar organizations or completely dissimilar organizations. You may also find that the business community does not connect formally, but rather informally. If you are struggling to create a list, consider asking local businesspeople how they connect with fellow businesses to share news, information, and support one another. You may find that they don't have a forum and that the library is just the place to establish one.

Contingent on your library's demographics, your list may be very long or short. Regardless of its size, it is important to pace yourself and set reasonable goals about forming these connections, otherwise it is easy to feel overwhelmed. Additionally, you have to think about your library's staff and project needs to ensure that they do not conflict. Take all of this into consideration when you prepare your list of organizations and formulate an action plan.

STEP 2

Reach Out to Contacts

Now that you have developed your network list, you can start reaching out to contacts by e-mail, phone, or in person. Keep in mind that whichever method(s) you choose, there are a few pros and cons to each one. To begin with, sometimes business owners feel overwhelmed or taken aback if you enter their business or call them unannounced. Alternatively, sending an e-mail may not prompt an urgency to respond or may get lost in their in-box. Remember to have patience; the small business community is limited on time and money so they typically do not have expendable staff or hours to respond to every e-mail or message that they receive. Therefore, you may want to approach your contact initially by e-mail and then follow up with a phone call or another e-mail.

It helps to start with a business owner or organization that you may already be acquainted with, even if it is only slightly. Not only may this bring you the confidence that you need to get this process started, but it is a great opportunity to build upon any relationship that you have already formed. Additionally, small business owners may share information and resources with fellow business owners so this may be what you need to make new contacts.

Regardless of how you decide to contact the business, organization, or person, it is important to assure them that this is not a major commitment. As you know by now, business owners and job seekers are limited on time and money and may be less enthusiastic about learning about the library when they are under the assumption that they will be obligated or committed to an ongoing process or partnership. For this reason, using the word *partnership* may be intimidating or overwhelming for the business community. Of course, after you have built a solid foundation together, you can certainly approach them about an ongoing partnership. In fact, these relationships will probably form naturally over time without ever using the word *partnership*. But for right now, remember that the purpose of making these initial contacts is to position yourself in the community by forming relationships that will be the foundation for future opportunities.

STEP 3

Develop a Presentation

Now that you have made a connection and set up an appointment, it is important to make it count so you have to go in prepared. Even if your contacts already frequent and appreciate the library, they may

---

Suggestion for Reaching Out to Network Contacts

Nothing complex, just short and simple: "Hi [business owner/organization], my name is [insert name] and I'm the business librarian at [library name]. I would really appreciate the opportunity to stop by your business to introduce myself and share a little bit about the library and learn more about your organization."

Some opportunities may be at a weekly or monthly meeting where you can be a guest speaker, or a brief meeting with the owner/manager/organizer. In terms of time, when in doubt, keep it short, about 15–20 minutes. It very well may (and probably will) go longer because they may have more questions for you or want to talk more about the library's services. If they offer you a full 30 minutes to an hour to talk, that's wonderful! But even 10 minutes is a perfect amount of time to introduce yourself.

simply be unaware that business resources and services are available there. This is your opportunity to really demonstrate that the library is a place that directly adds value and meaning to their life, business, and community.

Do your homework first. Refer back to your research that you completed about the business community, business trends, and any additional information about this particular organization/business/industry. While you will be learning more about them during your meeting, you also want to come in equipped with a presentation that is going to be relevant. Additionally, place an emphasis on aspects of the library's services that people are probably unaware of: meeting spaces, databases, computer training, workshops, and so on.

Some ideas for initial presentations include:

- Demonstration on creating prospective client lists
- Demonstration on creating prospective business-to-business lists
- Demonstration on industry reports
- Technology training, how to create a podcast or basic video
- Social media training
- Explanation of library space, meeting rooms, library cards, relevant resources, and staff duties

When you are giving your presentation, make it memorable by engaging them in the conversation rather than just talking at them. Include local business trivia, ask questions about what they enjoy most about the business community, and learn their start-up stories. Short and sweet can go a long way versus long, drawn-out presentations that lose people's interest.

STEP 4

Create a Call to Action

Once you have completed your presentation, the worst thing that you can do is to thank them for their time and just leave. While they may have truly enjoyed meeting you and learning more about the library, they may not have the initiative to follow up with you once they return to their busy schedules and commitments. Therefore, it is imperative that you create a follow-up opportunity that will make them want to reach out to you again.

In designing your follow-up opportunities, keep in mind that you may have to be creative in terms of when and where is convenient for your business community. This may mean stepping out of the traditional library box and meeting at a time or location that is not at the library or within traditional library hours.

Depending on your library and community, the following are some ideas to continue engagement:

Networking breakfast. This is hosted at the library, or other location. I have found that businesspeople prefer to meet in the morning before they have to open up shop or be in meetings all day.

Group training sessions. Offer to meet with their networking group, committee, or merchant group for social media, database instruction, video creation, and so on. As a side note, think about what unique talents you have that you haven't necessarily brought into the library before. Now is a good time to bring that into your business group. Maybe you like doing photography in your spare time and can show business owners the best type of lighting for photographing items. Or maybe you are great at creating websites—offer that training, too.

One-on-one appointments. If group training is not available, offer to set up appointments with business owners and professionals individually to discuss what library resources may benefit them and their business needs.

Video marketing or podcasting. Consider hosting a regular video series where the library provides video series to businesses that want to share their story with the community. Additionally, a podcast series is an easy way for local professionals and owners to share their expertise about entrepreneurship, management, leadership, and so on. Both of these can be hosted on the library website and on social media.

Future programs. Be sure to promote any upcoming workshops or programs that will be hosted at or through the library, and encourage attendance.

When you are offering these follow-up opportunities, you probably do not want to offer all of them at once. Especially in these beginning stages of forming connections, it is important to make options and opportunities as uncomplicated and simple as possible. Otherwise, many people will feel confused, uninspired, and inundated. Additionally, you will want to keep some of these other ideas on hand for future presentations and meetings.

Show your enthusiasm and excitement in the follow-up opportunities and show that you are genuinely interested in meeting them again. Make sure to offer the call to action within a week or two of your initial meeting so that attendees do not lose interest and excitement. The most important thing is to not let this initial meeting and presentation go to waste by not offering a call to action. If you lose this initial groundwork, it will be very hard to recover since you will lose the opportunity for an ongoing conversation and relationship.

At the end of your presentation, swap business cards (this means that you need to have your own) so that you can thank them for their time and send out reminder e-mails or an e-vite.

STEP 5

Network, Network, Network

You have successfully gone through your first round of navigating the business community. Now that you've completed it, is it time to retreat to the reference desk or hide in the library? No! In actuality, your work has just begun. All of these steps were simply a prelude to setting yourself up as the embedded business librarian. So now is the crucial time to keep the momentum going. The more comfortable you are networking, the more likely you are to convey a positive impression of the library and your desire to build relationships in the community.

It is important to communicate to your management team that you may go to networking events and pass out cards and nothing comes of it, and other times you have too many opportunities to count. However, one situation is not necessarily better than the other. They are both about putting face time into the community, building connections, getting experience, and putting yourself out there.

The basic principle is to not retreat, shy away, or lose traction. You've gained a solid amount of ground already, and this will help boost your confidence and position yourself as embedded in your community.

The business community knows one another and are willing to share referrals and make recommendations to their peers. Often business groups are looking for a new speaker or presenter at their monthly meetings.

Here are some recommendations for ways that you can network in the community:

- Open house events
- Ribbon cuttings
- Network scrambles
- Showcases and exhibits
- Workshops/events hosted at local businesses
- Check meetup.com for events and meetings
- Job fairs
- Chamber of Commerce events
- Village Hall merchant meetings
- Business committees
- Rotary Club or other professional groups
- Small Business Development Center (find your chapter here: https://www.sba.gov/tools/local-assistance/sbdc)

Q & A

When I am networking in the community, how should I introduce myself and explain what I do?

When you are developing your introductions and elevator speech, think about the skills that you provide, the workshops that you teach, and the research that you conduct. Librarians are educators, teachers, researchers, trainers, speakers, and so much more. However, when we simply say "I am a librarian who works with businesses," it doesn't necessarily convey the depth of our role and impact on the community.

Some tips to keep in mind as you go through this process and network:

- Have business cards ready to pass out—you'll need them. Also, don't be shy in asking for business cards from the people that you meet. As your business card collection grows, it is important to write notes on the back of them to help you stay organized.

- Have a traveling presentation prepared and ready to go on the fly. This will probably adapt and evolve as you discover what aspects of the library really piques the business community's interest, and you may also have several traveling presentations depending on which group you are talking to. But definitely have one ready that you can access right away by saving it to your Google Drive account or Dropbox so that you can access it anywhere with Wi-Fi for a last-minute request.

- The article "How to Tell People What You Do and Be Remembered" published by the Daily Muse is very helpful when formulating an introduction that counts (https://www.themuse.com/advice/how-to-tell-people-what-you-doand-be-remembered). The more that you network, the more confident you will be in your abilities and in the library's position in the business community. You will also learn how to answer questions and bring up subjects relevant to your library's community.

Not only is networking very important for developing your own confidence, but it is the single best way to really understand more about the business community, meet professionals, and learn about trends, strengths, opportunities, and goals and how the library fits into that equation. It also shows professionals that the library genuinely cares about the community and wants to be part of it as a valued voice, resource, and counterpart.

Five Steps to Embedded Business Librarianship

1. Create a networking list
2. Reach out to contacts
3. Develop a presentation
4. Create a call to action
5. Network, network, network

FINAL THOUGHTS

As you walk through this process, keep the core principles of becoming embedded in your library's business community at the forefront: this is not an opportunity to judge what you may assume the business community needs or to try and "solve" problems; this is a chance to build meaningful relationships. While you have done initial research on the business community, that was simply to gain a perspective and garner some ideas and topics for the library and your position. However, it does not give you the authority to seem to "know everything" and come in ready to solve problems and put out fires.

While the above steps are outlined in a format that can be easily understood and replicated, you have to be the one to determine what is best for you, the library, and your community. As a result, you may find through trial and error that one step works better than another. However, this lays the basic groundwork of what is expected in building connections with your library's business community. Above all, do not hesitate to think creatively or take on an initiative that seems out of the ordinary if it is something that the business community has expressed interest in.

Above all, use these meetings as opportunities to really listen to what the business community is experiencing as a whole, as well as each business member's unique story. Throughout these steps, you can be embedded by becoming an equitable ally to the business community and a valued resource, and to have the library not only be acknowledged, but respected and valued in the business community because you are actually listening to their needs and expressing interest in their journeys.

LET'S SUM IT UP

- When you meet with business owners, organizations, or committees, be open to learning more about them and how you want to work together.
- Developing follow-up opportunities is the best way to maintain contact with connections.
- Practice how you can explain to others what you do and why it matters.
- Continue networking and attending relevant events and gatherings to keep the momentum going.
- Take time to stop and listen to their perspectives on the business community.
- The five-step plan is simply the path to becoming embedded in your community. The work has just begun!

4

Networking with the Three Core Groups of the Business Community

IN THIS CHAPTER, WE WILL LEARN

- How to support small business owners

- New opportunities for developing relationships with professionals

- The best ways to support the job-seeker community

You have successfully created an action plan for navigating your business community. Now it is time to continue networking and approaching various organizations, businesses, and professionals for collaboration opportunities. As you navigate your library's business community through committee participation, attending meetings and events, and making connections through consistent involvement, you will encounter people with a variety of needs, interests, strengths, and opportunities. At times, the types of businesses and professionals in your community may seem limitless and confusing. However, you will probably notice that the business community can be divided into three distinct categories: small business owners, professionals, and job seekers.

Throughout your interactions and research, we know that these three groups all have one core commonality: they are limited in their time and money. However, that knowledge does not mean that each group should be approached and connected with in the same way. Rather, the individuals, businesses, and organizations within the groups are unique. Therefore, it is imperative to continue navigating the business community so that you can truly build meaningful relationships that will transform your connections. As a result, each group deserves its own tailored services and interactions.

In this chapter, we will discuss the characteristics of small business owners, professionals, and job seekers and how you can uniquely engage and support them.

SMALL BUSINESS OWNERS

According to the U.S. Small Business Association, small businesses may be small, but they have a huge impact on our economy. Take a look at some of these statistics.[1]

- Since 1982, there has been a 49 percent increase in small businesses.
- Small businesses are responsible for adding eight million new jobs to the economy since 1990, while big business has eliminated four million jobs.
- There are about 28 million small businesses in the United States that account for 54 percent of all U.S. sales.

Consider your own community's small business demographics. In the research we did in chapter 3, "Navigating the Business Community," you probably looked up the demographics for small businesses in your area. In essence, small businesses could be responsible for the majority of our community members' salaries and careers. This inevitably impacts the growth and sustainability of the library's community. When the library supports small businesses, it sends a strong message: the library is invested in the progress and livelihood of its community.

Indeed, many libraries do have relationships with the small businesses in their area. However, this relationship may be solely based on taking rather than giving. As librarians, particularly those in management, it is imperative that we ask ourselves when was the last time we supported our local businesses without an assumption that they would support us back. Think about the last time that your library needed sponsors for a summer reading club or a donation: you may have gone to your small business community. Perhaps you asked for a donation, financial or otherwise, and in exchange you put their logo on your library's newsletter and website. Was this the extent of your relationship with the business?

Alternatively, think about the last time that your library approached the small businesses in your community and offered them training or a service with no expectation of something in return. To clarify, this is not to say that small businesses are opposed to supporting their local library. In fact, small businesses are often exceedingly generous in their donations to the library with no expectation of publicity. This is because small business owners care about the progress of their community. The library is and should be no different.

If we want to show that the library unequivocally supports small business owners, we need to shift our communication strategy. The focus should be on how the library can support its community's local businesses. This does not necessarily mean simply patronizing their restaurants when you and your colleagues go out to lunch, but demonstrating in a meaningful way that the library is their cheerleader and cares deeply about their success. In the previous chapter, we discussed the five steps to navigating your library's business community. Now that you are an expert on these five steps, we are going to bring them to small businesses.

The small business community is typically very social and active; they lean on one another for support, encouragement, advice, and assistance. As the embedded business librarian, you will be focused on engaging with small business owners through consistent and regular communication in their networking circles. Although every community is unique, you may find that you spend the majority of your time networking with small business owners instead of job seekers or professionals. Because job seekers and professionals may be limited in the time that they can spend in the community depending on their schedules, small business owners may comprise the largest percentage of your interactions with the business community.

As outlined in your action plan, you may develop relationships with small business owners by hosting training sessions at their staff meetings, visiting their local businesses and learning more about the services they provide, collaborating with them on a community initiative, or cohosting a networking event. In your consistent and ongoing relationships with small business owners, you will be able to determine where the library can step in.

Q & A

What is the difference between "entrepreneurs" and "small business owners"?

Often, the terms *entrepreneur* and *small business owner* are used synonymously, and some may argue that there is no difference between them. In fact, in an article in the *Wall Street Journal*, experts and readers weighed in on their opinions about "small business owners" versus "entrepreneurs." Some descriptions stated that entrepreneurs focus on current and future market trends and are more likely to take risks, while small business owners have a goal of growing a business that can "support themselves and their families [with] no intentions of growing it much more."[*] You will definitely encounter individuals who refer to themselves as "entrepreneurs" and network in entrepreneur and small business circles.

* Kelly K. Spors, "Is a Small-Business Owner Always an Entrepreneur?" *Wall Street Journal,* September 16, 2008, www.wsj.com/articles/SB122153790674841873.

Initially, you probably will feel like an outsider in your interactions with the business community. That's okay. The key is to stay consistently involved. As your connections and partnerships with small business owners deepen, the following core communication points can guide you:

Stay impartial. The wonderful aspect about becoming embedded in your library's business community is that you will be seen as a trusted source and partner. However, sometimes that means that individuals may want to get you involved in local business politics. Throughout your interactions with small business owners in meetings, committees, and networking events, you may learn about conflicts within the business community. Whether it is between rival businesses, individuals, or relationships with Chamber of Commerce members or town or village ordinances, it is absolutely essential that you do not get involved. As a representative of the library, it is your responsibility to lend your support and encouragement to all areas of the business community and all business owners without creating alliances.

Don't be a hero. It can be deceptively easy to want to become your small business community's superhero and solve all of their problems. Particularly in the beginning, small business owners may be in awe of the wealth of information and knowledge that you can provide and therefore may increasingly approach you asking for advice and solutions. In fact, you may feel inclined or pressured to solve every problem presented to you. From the outset it is important to refrain from offering too many solutions. To begin with, you cannot assume that you truly understand their struggles and problems and have an arsenal of remedies for every quandary. Secondly, you need to remind yourself that your role as an embedded business librarian is to support small business owners to the best of your ability.

Sometimes you truly do not have a solution or an answer and you have to remind yourself that that is okay. Thirdly, in connecting with small business owners, demonstrating your support for them, and creating a platform for them to connect with other business owners, you will hopefully assist them in finding solutions collaboratively. It is not your responsibility to solve all problems. Being embedded does not mean you bear the brunt of their struggles.

Be an equal voice. Always remember that the ultimate goal in being embedded in your library's business community is to be their equal partner and an active voice. Some days you may need to step back and remind yourself that you are aiming to be seen as a valued voice at the table and to remain impartial. Your focus is on building transformational relationships by being a fellow colleague.

PROFESSIONALS

For the purpose of this book, the term *professionals* is used to describe anyone in your community who plays a role in the economic cycle as part of their career. While this term may have a broad spectrum, it can be broken into different professional areas. For example, educators, management consultants, and financial advisors may be considered professionals because of their level of education or skill, while doctors, lawyers, realtors, and accountants may also be considered professionals, but could have their own private practice. Regardless of their type of employment, they have a profound impact on the business community. When connecting with the professionals in your business community, you may notice that it is more difficult to make initial connections and to assess their needs. To begin with, the amount of time that they spend within the community, particularly in the business community, is dependent on their work schedule. Additionally, they may have little to no relationship with the library except for occasionally stopping in. This is a key example of why it is so imperative to be embedded in your library's business community; you may not meet professionals at the same locations or during the same times as small business owners.

Furthermore, professionals have a variety of needs due to their various industries, positions, and projects. Therefore, it is essential not to assume that they always have similar goals or aspirations. In fact, a professional who works for a large corporation may not necessarily be interested in learning the basics of social media marketing if it is not directly important to their position. They may, however, be interested in creating prospective business or client lists.

As an embedded business liaison, you will be tasked with thinking of new ways to find out what is the best service model for your community. I worked in a community where there was a significant group of parents who were severely limited on travel because their spouses used the car to get to work and public transportation was unreliable. In this situation, my colleague and I made arrangements with local apartment complexes to host a simultaneous story time and computer instruction courses in the complexes' community rooms. My colleague, a youth services librarian, engaged the children in story time and crafts while I brought a couple of laptops from the library and taught the adults basic computer instruction and how to access the library's website and databases. The point of this anecdote is to encourage you to not be afraid of situations that seem impossible.

Again, while the goals and aspirations of professionals in your community will be dependent on their career and position, professionals typically respond well to the following workshops, trainings, and discussions:

- Sales generation
- Marketing
- Client lists
- Business-to-business research
- Industry and company profiles

You will be able to teach yourself many of these topics based on library resources and databases that you have available. For other

Q & A

It's easier for me to meet small business owners.
How can I get recognized among the professionals
in my public library's community?

As stated earlier, where and how you meet professionals will be as various as they are. Unlike small business owners who typically network and associate within the same organizations and groups, professionals may or may not be found within the business community. They may, however, be very active in their children's sports team, their house of worship, or the school's PTA. Furthermore, they may simply not be active in extracurricular commitments, but enjoy going to the local farmer's market or street festivals. This is where it will be more difficult, and having a foundational relationship with local businesses can help you greatly. Some suggestions for reaching this group include:

1. Ask your colleagues to pass out your business cards during their own outreach initiatives with local schools, book clubs, cultural centers, and so on.
2. Ask local community colleges, shopping centers, gyms, and businesses that you have developed relationships with to pass along library information.
3. In the library's newsletter and on the library's social media pages, advertise who you are, what services you provide, and how professionals can get in contact with you.
4. Submit a press release to the local newspaper about how you can support professionals in the area, as well as the type of resources that the library provides.
5. Contribute to the library's social media presence about business resources, activities, and your expertise.

Particularly in the beginning, this will feel more like outreach rather than embedded business librarianship. But as you become more connected with your library's business community, you will learn about more opportunities to connect with professionals in a meaningful way. Think of these steps as the actions that you have to take on your path toward becoming embedded.

topics you will need to partner with local experts, organizations, and business owners. In the following chapter, we will discuss ways to implement training and workshops in the library.

As you start developing relationships with the professionals in your community, consider these points:

You are an information specialist. You may be questioned by professionals as to how you are qualified to help them with business or about the credibility of the business resources that you recommend. Alternatively, you may also be misunderstood as a personal assistant or business guru. This is when it is important to remind yourself and your connections that you are an information specialist who is simply introducing them to resources that may help them with their career. However, it is up to them to actually decide whether or not to use these tools. This means that it is not your job to actually do their research or projects, but rather to guide them.

One-on-one appointments. Perhaps the most effective way that you will be able to connect with professionals is through one-on-one appointments. These are excellent opportunities where you can introduce them to the resources, databases, and information that they will be able to access from their office. Consider hosting open office hours in the evening or on weekends when they have more availability.

Webinars and virtual training. Since professionals may not be able to travel outside of the office during the day, it is beneficial to have training resources available for remote access. Create a Slideshare account with step-by-step instructions to the library's business databases or upload a video tutorial playlist. Furthermore, experiment with a webinar by utilizing Google Hangouts/Google Hangouts On Air to broadcast database tutorials for free.

Professionals are a unique group because their industries can vary greatly, and getting in touch with them can be very difficult. However, by continuing to form connections in the community and experimenting with new ways to provide training, you will learn more about this group and how you can build transformational relationships.

JOB SEEKERS

If people thought libraries were obsolete, the Great Recession proved just how valuable libraries can be, especially to job seekers. According to a report, *Job-Seeking in U.S. Public Libraries* by the American Library Association and the Information Policy & Access Center (University of Maryland), online classes for job seekers increased by 20 percent from 2009 to 2011.[2] Furthermore, a 2013 study conducted by the Pew Research Center found that "47% of job seekers say help finding or applying for a job is 'very important' to them and their families."[3] Clearly there is a significant amount of evidence that shows that libraries are centers that are valuable for job seekers.

As librarians, we can revolutionize their job search strategy. Typically job seekers submit resumes through online job search engines. However, they have a stronger job search strategy if they employ the other resources that the library offers, including industry profiles, company lists, SWOT analyses, skills training, and resume/cover letter assistance. Additionally, while you may already have individuals who come into the library asking for job and computer assistance, there is a solid percentage of individuals who do not even consider the library as a resource. The paradox is that while this group may not consider utilizing their local library, they are the very group that could benefit the most from the databases, information, and specialists available at the library.

You can certainly host job-seeker courses and workshops at the library, but consider building connections and partnerships with local organizations that are already making valiant efforts with the unemployed. Together, you can combine expertise and resources to create a dynamic job-seeker support system. The job-seeker group, above all others, is probably the one with individuals who are most pressed on time and money. It is our duty to provide them with the valuable information that they need as efficiently as possible.

If you want to connect with job seekers and develop sustainable relationships with them, follow your action plan and make connections with organizations that support job seekers. Each community will have its own unique organizations and support systems, but some suggestions include the following:

- *Faith-based employment ministries.* Often there are groups that meet regularly at houses of worship for support and job-seeker guidance.
- *American Job Centers* (find your local chapter here: www.careeronestop.org/localhelp/find-american-job -centers.aspx).
- *Community colleges.* Many community colleges have job-seeker support groups and continuing job skills divisions that partner with local job centers.
- *Community park districts.* Park districts frequently host job seeker workshops or resume assistance services.
- If there are simply no viable options in your community, consider starting a job-seekers club by partnering with another organization, school, or business. You can also advertise through Meetup.com or the Chamber of Commerce to reach beyond your current patron base.

As your relationships with organizations that help job seekers expand, you will be able to find out what the needs of the users and the organizations are. Teaching a regular class outside of the library is an excellent way to start introducing job seekers who otherwise may not utilize the library databases and resources that can assist them in their job search. While you may be able to teach them basic job search strategies, also consider providing instruction on the resources that are unique to library databases. Some of these topics include:

- Resources for editing resumes and cover letters
- Resources for improving computer and social media abilities

- Creating customized prospective business lists
- Researching industry reports
- Creating SWOT (Strengths, Weaknesses, Opportunities, and Threats) analyses of companies
- Learning about industry trends in the news and social media

Perhaps an option for you would be teaching a class twice a month at a local organization or developing a class presentation that you can share with individuals so that they can access the training from home and at their own pace. Additionally, you can make yourself available for individual appointments. Whichever option you choose, the key to providing quality job-seeker assistance is consistency and sustainability so that you can develop a reputation as a valued resource for job seekers.

As with small business owners and professionals, you must know how to interact with job seekers in a way that will be beneficial to them. This is where it is important and necessary to set some ground rules:

You are not their job coach. As a librarian and information specialist, your role is to introduce them to the resources and databases that have the ability to take their career search to the next level. However, you do not provide job advice about specific companies, industries, resumes, promotions, salary negotiations, and so on. As with your interactions with small business owners and professionals, it is important for you to stay impartial.

Know your limits. There is a key difference between meeting with a job seeker and helping them learn computer skills or how to navigate a database versus actually doing their job research. As a librarian, you are not responsible for filling out private information, and this includes job applications and editing cover letters and resumes. If you feel that someone needs more assistance than you are able to provide, recommend him or her to a local organization that can assist them. In situations like this, you will find that developing a relationship with another job-seeker group in the area is especially helpful for referring job seekers to one another.

Bring in the experts. Many job-seeker workshops and programs at the library can be staff-led since they are instructional and informational. However, there are times when you do need to bring in experts who can provide training on negotiating salaries, interview preparation, and networking recommendations. Do not be afraid to partner with people in your community, particularly business owners and consultants, who can share their knowledge.

FINAL THOUGHTS

In your navigation of the business community, you will likely find that small business owners, professionals, and job seekers are the three core groups with which you will build transformational relationships. However, each group has different needs and goals. Therefore, the way that you approach, communicate, and provide services to each group should be unique. This means that you will probably interact with small business owners and entrepreneurs, professionals, and job seekers in different environments.

Depending on your library's previous relationship with the business community, this may mean taking on a drastically different approach to offering services with no expectation in return.

LET'S SUM IT UP

- Business owners, professionals, and job seekers all have a variety of needs. You will need to approach each group uniquely with their best interests in mind.

- Consider how you can start supporting local businesses without expectations of receiving donations or other type of support in return.

- You'll need to use ingenuity to reach out to professionals who may not come to the library or are difficult to meet in the community.

- Partnering with local job-seeker organizations can help you consistently reach those who are in career transition.

- As you develop relationships and connections, recognize what you are able to do in this position and what is beyond your scope of responsibility.

NOTES

1. "Small Business Trends: Small Business, Big Impact!" U.S. Small Business Administration, September 7, 2015, https://www.sba.gov/content/small-business-trends-impact.

2. "Public Library Funding & Technology Access Study 2011–2012" (n.d.), American Library Association, www.ala.org/research/plftas/2011_2012.

3. K. Zickuhr, L. Rainie, K. Purcell, and M. Duggan, "How Americans Value Public Libraries in Their Communities," Pew Research Center, December 11, 2013, http://libraries.pewinternet.org/2013/12/11/libraries-in-communities.

5
Bringing It Back to the Library

IN THIS CHAPTER, WE WILL LEARN

- The power of networking events and how you can incorporate them into your library's programming

- Workshops and training sessions that add value to members of the business community, as well as form lasting relationships with the library

- Ongoing programs and initiatives that can be utilized among the business community throughout the year

- How developing a coworking space at the library can create a welcoming environment for members of the business community

You have really stepped up the opportunities to network and reach out to the business community and its professionals, business owners, and job seekers. In being embedded in the business community, you have no doubt learned more about their opportunities, strengths, and challenges. The wonderful part of being an equal voice outside of the library means that you have a unique perspective of where the business owners, job seekers, and professionals stand in positions and companies. This not only helps you continue to develop more meaningful relationships outside of the library, but it also gives you great insight into where the library can meet their needs within the library. The responses and information that you receive from the business community can provide feedback to your colleagues and help you understand where the library's strengths and areas of improvement are in terms of the programming, resources, databases, and structure of the library.

The other added benefit of building relationships in the community means that you have a new avenue for publicizing your events and the library's attributes. In the past, you may have limited yourself to advertising these events in the library newsletter, calendar, and social media. Through your relationships in the community, you will now be able to encourage individuals to attend, bring their colleagues or peers, and also get personalized feedback about what is working and what is not working.

In this chapter, we are going to discuss ways that you can encourage the business community to come into the library and, specifically, how you can tailor programming and create an environment that encourages collaboration, education, and learning for members of the business community.

You will probably be asked to do events and programs that are completely different from what you have done in the past. In your role as embedded business librarian, you will be getting comfortable, if you haven't already, with change, trying new endeavors, and doing programs and projects that are out of the box. Programming and creating a collaborative environment are no different.

A final note about bringing the business community back into the library: this is the area that you may want to explore *after* you have started to solidify your role in the business community as an embedded business librarian. It may be tempting to do programming and rethink coworking spaces first, but initially building those relationships in the community can help you truly understand how the library can help.

NETWORKING EVENTS

Throughout your interactions as the embedded business librarian, you are no doubt socializing and collaborating with various parts of the business community that may not know about one another. The work that you do with the professionals may be different from the work that you have done with the small business owners. Additionally, the job seekers may just be completely out of the loop. Hosting a networking event at the library serves you, the library, and the business community—there are major positive occurrences that can result from this.

To begin with, when you host a networking event at the library, you are introducing members of the entire business community— business owners, professionals, and job seekers—to connect both with the library and with each other. Secondly, you are solidifying your role as a person in the community who genuinely cares about the well-being and progress of the residents. And finally, the impact of placing the library at the center of these connections is priceless. These individuals will not only think of their library as a place with helpful staff and resources, but also as a place that literally brings the community together.

If you decide to host a networking event at the library, here are some guided suggestions to make it a success.

Networking breakfast. Often, members of the business community simply do not have time in the afternoon or after work for an added commitment. Mornings can be the optimal time for people to meet since they are not yet caught up in their hectic schedules or work commitments. Host the breakfast in the morning, before the library opens. This event will last about one and a half hours.

The first thirty minutes can be a continental breakfast with networking, followed by a presentation by you about upcoming events at the library, resources they may not have heard about, and how they can obtain a library card. You can also include a brief demonstration of a database, and a tour of the library space and any equipment or material that is particularly beneficial to them.

For this event, you may need to recruit fellow colleagues to help out with organizing the event, offering tours, socializing with the attendees, passing out newsletters, and registering individuals for library cards. Additionally, you may want to advertise this event in your library's newsletter, e-news, and social media, but also promote it in the local newspaper, at local Chamber of Commerce, village, or committee meetings, and send out individual invitations.

Lunch and Learn networking. Similar to a networking breakfast, but shorter, this event would either provide lunch or be a brown-bag lunch for professionals who want to network and also receive a demonstration about a database or library resources that can be beneficial to them and their professional endeavors. This event requires much less staff time and coordination than the networking breakfast.

Networking tutorials. Host a program or workshop conducted by an expert on business and networking etiquette. This will bring individuals in who will be able to learn how to effectively and professionally network in the business world, while also creating an environment for people to meet and greet with one another. Encourage attendees to bring their business cards.

Networking book discussions/community conversations. Host an event in the community, at a restaurant or bar, that encourages professionals to come and discuss a book or business-related topic. While not in the library, it is a library-sponsored program. The library can purchase the appetizers while drinks and meals are available for individual purchase. Partner with another networking group or organization to cross-promote this event. Additionally, ask the restaurant or bar to promote the event on their social media. Encourage members of the business community to come out and support a local business while meeting new people.

Networking events hosted by the group. This is the least time-consuming of all of these options. Encourage groups and businesses to host their meetings and events in the library meeting room space and simply ask if you can stop in for 5–10 minutes to welcome them, introduce yourself, and share some information about the library and your role that they may find useful. While this is not a program hosted through the library, it is an easy way for you to get professionals into the library and interacting with your space.

Office Hours. The most informal of networking programs, this is an opportunity for you to host a drop-in networking event where individuals can come to a designated space in the library, work on their projects, learn about new business resources, ask for your guidance, and meet fellow business members. Create a coffee-hour atmosphere where people feel that this is the space for them to get some work done casually and make new acquaintances.

TRAINING

In your interactions with the business community, you will learn about the resources and information that they need. The training classes you undertake in response can be self-taught or taught in collaboration with a colleague to make them more effective. Continue to learn what types of resources the business community uses and how you can support them through training both in the library and off-site. Training programs not only bring individuals into the library, but also showcase the databases, books, and equipment that the library has that they can utilize. Many of these trainings can be collaborated with the networking events listed above, specifically the Lunch and Learns and Office Hours events. This may help in attracting more attendance and a wider audience.

Create prospective business-to-business lists. Many small business owners need to know how to do business-to-business sales or find out what other business trends are. Additionally, they may be interested in expanding their business to another community.

Social media. Popular social media for the business community include Facebook, Twitter, Pinterest, LinkedIn, Instagram, and YouTube. Workshops can include individualized classes for each social media platform, explaining social media concepts like hashtags, purpose, structure, and organization, or themed classes like preparing a social media action plan for the summer and holidays or for unveiling new products. Additionally, for job seekers, you can do work a workshop about building up a valuable web presence.

Apps. Vine, Snapchat, Instagram, and Periscope are just some of the apps that could be new and trendy for businesses that want to engage in marketing to younger, smartphone-friendly audiences. Again, this workshop could discuss each app individually or go through an overview of all of the apps, how they are used, and how they can be tailored to a business's marketing strategy. For programming, apps are also an easy way to host informal networking opportunities, like through the library's Office Hours event mentioned above.

Blog/website creation. Introduce individuals to how they can create a website or a blog using Squarespace, Weebly, WordPress, Blogger, Tumblr, or other platforms. Discuss how they can create a website, the elements that go into a successful website or blog, and how they can promote their products and services by creating an online web presence.

Taking business online, including Etsy for Beginners. This workshop would be beneficial for artisans and crafty individuals who want to build a platform for selling their products online. Additionally, it can be useful for any small business that wants to grow its business and services onto an online platform. Unless you have specific experience with Etsy, you may want to call in a professional who has had significant experience or success using this platform.

Podcasts. Podcasts are a relatively easy way for individuals to share their stories with the community and build a following. Podcasts can help people who have a unique story to tell or want a different way to promote their business or expertise. Workshops can include how to use GarageBand, Audacity, iTunes, and SoundCloud. If the library has equipment (laptops, microphone, software) that the patrons can use, they can also learn about how this equipment can be checked out with their library card. Furthermore, you can host a drop-in or ongoing program where you ask individuals to participate in a podcast series that the library hosts. They can get an idea of how a podcast would be conducted and how they can incorporate library space or materials.

Video tutorials. Similarly to podcasts, you can host a workshop about how to use video camera equipment or what the elements are for a successful video that the business can create on its own. If your library hosts an ongoing video series that showcases business and community stories, give examples of what has worked well for the library and what has not worked well. Furthermore, you can host an event where members of the business community can participate in community conversation videos at a program at the library.

Maker events. If your library has maker equipment, like a 3D printer, laser cutter, vinyl cutter, or other material, host an event about how the business community can utilize these resources. If your library does not have access to maker equipment, you can still do maker-geared events that include simple crafts, redesigns, or innovations. Host these tutorials or instructional sessions or create them as drop-in events with instructions posted so that they can be self-paced. Great ideas can be found at http://makeitatyourlibrary.org.

Miscellaneous tech. Share information that your business community may need to learn more about creating and using Gmail, creating infographics for presentations, and using Skype or Google Hangouts for web calls or virtual presentations.

COLLABORATIVE PROGRAMS

As librarians, we are multiskilled and talented. We are capable of teaching a wide variety of workshops and classes. However, some topics are ones that are not in our realm of expertise:

- Intellectual property protection
- Legal issues for business owners and employers
- Tax issues for business owners
- Bookkeeping, particularly training with programs like QuickBooks
- Public speaking advice
- Marketing strategies
- Sales techniques
- Buying a franchise
- Cash flow management
- Interviewing and salary negotiation advice

Q & A

What is the best way to handle business owners and professionals who want to use the library as a platform to increase their sales?

Throughout your interactions, you will encounter local business community members who would like to do programs at the library. However, there may be some professionals who want to do programming at the library in order to boost their client portfolio or sales generation. This should not be within the library's offerings. When contracting outside programmers for the library, it is imperative to be clear and direct with potential programmers, as well as to utilize a contract. To begin with, in areas concerning finances and health, partner with organizations whose aim is to provide enriching resources and information with no expectation of generating clients or boosting sales numbers. Some recommendations of organizations to partner with include:

- County health departments
- Centers on health and aging
- Small Business Administration
- Community colleges
- Local career centers/resource centers

Find more local government organizations by state and filter to community assistance and development programs: https://www.usa.gov/local-governments#item-211680.

Utilizing the connections that you make in your business community for programming can be wonderful and a great addition to your offerings, while also bringing in unique ideas and new people to the library. Just cover these points of discussion so that those who do attend are left feeling like they learned something valuable and were not given a commercial or sales pitch.

Suggestions for Partnering with Presenters and Speakers for Library Programs

For all programs that you have at the library, including those from business owners or professionals, it is highly recommended to clearly state the nature of the programming through a verbal and written contract. Some pointers include:

- Programming is informational, not commercial
- Discussion of if and when they can pass out business cards or brochures
- Discussion about generating sales on library property restrictions
- Discussion of whether or not they can ask for e-mail addresses or contact information of attendees
- Discussion of ensuring that the information that is presented is factually based

As long as you use caution when partnering with anyone, particularly in regards to finances, legal, and health, as well as utilize a contract and provide clear and open discussion about the programming at the library, this should be straightforward and serve as an asset to the library, the patrons, and the community.

COLLABORATIVE WORKING ENVIRONMENT

You may have found out how many small business owners exist in your area, how many people are in a career transition, and what type of profession is the most prevalent. In your initial research and collaboration with the business community, you may or may not have come across "solopreneurs." By definition, solopreneurs are individuals who operate their business completely on their own.[1] This means that they do not have a traditional office space or brick-and-mortar storefront. Their business may be completely out of their own home, completely online, or a combination of both. The rise of solopreneurs is palpable. In 2011 there were 12.5 million solopreneurs, and in 2014 there were 17.9 million. This growth does not show any sign of slowing down, especially as the Internet is constantly allowing for new ways for individuals to connect with one another.[2] Furthermore, you may have professionals in your area who work for other companies, but their work is conducted remotely. Again, they do not have a traditional office to go work in. Since traditional work is becoming less common and career transitions are becoming more fluid, there is no doubt that the number of professionals working remotely will continue to increase.

Nevertheless, these trends create a valuable opportunity for the library. Because solopreneurs and professionals working remotely do not have traditional stores and office space, they are in a unique position of being able to work wherever they want. Working solo can be lonely, so many choose to work at coffee shops or public spaces. Coworking spaces are becoming more and more popular as this type of work spreads and the need to have a place where they can work among fellow solopreneurs and remote professionals also increases.

COWORKING SPACES

To begin with, coworking spaces are shared workspaces where entrepreneurs and professionals can work, meet, collaborate, and network. Sometimes coworking spaces have a specific niche and are geared toward fashion designers, tech professionals, artists, photographers, or chefs. Other spaces are more general and available for anyone to utilize. Often coworking environments have conference rooms, mini "offices," desks, and even kitchens, gyms, and showers so that they can feel like a true environment that people can utilize at any time.

So, why does this matter to public libraries? Coworking spaces indicate several important aspects about our economy and workforce as a whole and what we can expect for the future: they show the prominence of individuals who are electing to work in fields that are not traditional, as well as individuals who are using their own resources and talents to become their own boss. As the maker movement continues to be more accessible with open software and more affordable equipment, the job force will no doubt continue to adapt.

Most importantly, this information demonstrates the need and desire for people to work in public spaces and community centers. And secondly, it shows how public libraries can adapt to new technology and the maker movement by providing a platform for people to create, design, and learn. This indicates an opportunity for "communal creativity,"[3] and the public library is the perfect space for this philosophy. Because public libraries often still have a reputation for

Q & A

How can librarians adjust the public library to be more adaptable for coworking spaces?

To begin with, do research about what draws people to coworking spaces in the first place. If there are coworking spaces near your library, visit them so that you can get a feel for the environment and the resources that coworking spaces make available. If you do not have the ability to visit a coworking space, take a look online to see what is trending. Here are some suggested resources:

- 16 Cool Co-working Spaces (www.inc.com/ss/christina -desmarais/16-cool-coworking-spaces.html)
- The Top 100 Co-working Spaces in the U.S. (www.symmetry50 .com/blog/2015/5/13/the-top-100-coworking-spaces-in-the-us)
- Co-working Spaces (www.deskmag.com/encoworking-spaces)

Aside from kitchens, gyms, and showers, the greater part of coworking spaces can be adapted in the library. Given the meeting rooms, computer areas, and technology that you have available at your public library, the philosophy of a coworking environment can be readily implemented. Here are some suggestions for how you can create space that will encourage solopreneurs and remote professionals to come to your library:

Space. Coworking spaces leave room for working side-by-side and also individually. What does the space in your library look like? Are there tables that can be pushed together or are they mostly study carousels? If you cannot rearrange any furniture, consider having a regular coworking time in a meeting room where the tables are mixed or pushed together or are separated so that people can come in during a designated time to work together or work among their peers.

Quiet rules. Reconsider your library's rules on cell phone usage, playing music, or being quiet in general. Again, perhaps you can designate a specific area of the library or time of day where professionals can work together without volume restrictions.

Speakers/presentations. Many coworking spaces have Lunch and Learn events where they will have industry professionals present on a trendy topic. Additionally, they may have "show-and-tell," where the coworking space attendees share what they have been working on and get feedback from others. Consider hosting an event where people can "show off" their latest creations, business models, and projects.

Open lab. If your library has access to equipment or software, host an open lab where professionals can come in, learn about the technology, and create. This will be a good opportunity for them to learn more about the lesser-known resources at the library and see how they can implement them into their own practice.

Networking. Whether it is through a set program or something passive, find ways that members of the business community can network with one another at the library. Some coworking spaces have a wall with snapshots and fun trivia provided by individuals who utilize the space. Another idea is to host an ongoing podcast or video series that highlights the solopreneurs who come into the library. A major reason why coworking spaces are so attractive is because they offer ways for people to work together instead of in isolation.

being quiet, non-collaborative, outdated spaces, it is important that we change that image. Perhaps solopreneurs and remote professionals would be interested in working at their local library—after all, it is free, but they simply do not think that it will be amenable to their needs.

COWORKING SPACES IN ACTION

Two examples of successful coworking spaces include NaperLaunch at the Naperville Public Library in Naperville, Illinois, and The Co-working Connection at the Arlington Heights Memorial Library in Arlington Heights, Illinois.

Kent Palmer, business librarian at the Naperville Public Library, describes NaperLaunch as a designated space for collaborative coworking and for business events hosting up to thirty attendees. Advertised on Meetup.com, every Thursday there is an event at NaperLaunch. One Thursday per month the presentations are focused on teaching business owners how to make a presentation, present sales and funding pitches, and converse with potential business partners. The remaining Thursdays are focused on round table discussions regarding topics like e-commerce businesses, tech sectors, service businesses, and more. On the occasional fifth Thursday per month, NaperLaunch hosts pitch sessions where participants can practice making a funding or sales pitch while getting feedback from local bankers and investors who serve as judges for these pitch sessions.

Palmer, who has been business librarian at Naperville Public Library since 2012, also describes the implementation of a new program called NaperLaunch Academy in partnership with local qualified instructors. With eight to twelve participants per session, this initiative acts as an accelerator by providing established business owners with a higher level of instruction to increase their profits, business size, and more. Each session meets every two weeks for a total of twelve meetings with a combination of instruction and mastermind round table work.

Palmer explains that when the NaperLaunch space is not being used for events, it serves as a coworking space where ten to twenty business owners, professionals, and job seekers stop in regularly to work both collaboratively and independently.

At the Arlington Heights Memorial Library, Julie Kittredge, business services advisor, and Shannon Distel, specialty info services manager, have been hosting and expanding The Co-working Connection since 2015. In addition to a designated space in the library for members of the business community to work, collaborate, and access relevant resources, computers, and databases, every third Wednesday, the Business Services team hosts a structured informational and networking event. The original concept began with a regular open-ended event for networking and sharing each other's projects, but Kittredge and Distel have evolved this into a more tailored regular meeting. This includes a brief demonstration of a database or explanation of a resource, like how to find images for blogging or creating social media posts, in conjunction with a designated time frame for networking and collaborating with others. The purpose of the events is to provide value and a key takeaway for those in attendance, in conjunction with the opportunity to meet fellow professionals and entrepreneurs.

FINAL THOUGHTS

In this chapter, we discussed how you can take the information and connections that you are forming outside of the library and bring them back. So many times you will see how you can connect and collaborate within the business community, whether at a networking event, committee, or group meetings. However, it is important to also find ways that the business community can come into the library and learn more about the resources and opportunities there.

In designing your programs and rethinking your actual library space, keep in mind that the most important way to draw the business community into the library is the idea of networking and learning from and with one another. No amount of tools, books, or databases that the library possesses will bring people into the library unless they feel that it is a space where they can truly find, add, and create value.

Like so many aspects of this role, you will no doubt discover that the programming and environment you create at the library will be different and possibly intimidating. It may go against what the library has done in the past, but it may also be exactly what the business community needs to realize that their public library supports their future.

LET'S SUM IT UP

- Networking events at the library create an opportunity for the local business community to connect while learning the value of the library.
- Training and ongoing initiatives develop resources for the business community while directing them to the information and people that they need.
- The amount of "solopreneuers" is on the rise, as well as coworking spaces. The library can make major or minor adjustments to meet the needs of local entrepreneurs.

NOTES

1. Kate Taylor, "The Difference between a Solopreneur and a Side-Gigger (Infographic)," *Entrepreneur*, November 9, 2014, www.entrepreneur.com/article/239522.
2. Chad Brooks, "'Solopreneurs' Redefining Work," *Business News Daily*, October 7, 2014, www.businessnewsdaily.com/7246-freelance-workers-solopreneurs.html.
3. Derek Thompson, "A World without Work," *Atlantic*, July 1, 2015: 53.

6
The Embedded Business Librarian as Liaison

IN THIS CHAPTER, WE WILL LEARN

- How to incorporate embedded librarianship to fit your library's staff size and schedule

- How the liaison aspect of your job description makes your embedded library services available to all

- The best ways to navigate tricky situations with ease

As you get to know your library's business community, it is necessary for you to determine where your time and energy are best spent. As we discussed earlier, being embedded means that you recognize that you cannot be all things to all people. Similarly, it is imperative that you analyze and decide where and in what capacity you will concentrate your time and energy in order to be of optimal service to business owners, professionals, and job seekers.

Q & A

How can we adjust our staff schedule to make this work in our library?

Contingent on your schedule and library staffing needs, you will need to adjust how you are embedded in your library community. Perhaps you may only be able to teach a class at a career center twice a month but you may have more time set aside to hold individual appointments with job seekers. Or you may be in a situation where you will have to narrow down which business organizations you can serve on a committee with, and then make yourself available to speak or attend other business functions on a regular basis without a long-term commitment. The point is that only you and your library staff can determine what is the best use for your own time and your library's staff schedule and staff time.

As a library professional who has worked in several libraries of different staff sizes and budgets, as well as collaborated with librarians of various communities, I can relate to feeling overwhelmed or frustrated in wanting to do more for your community with limited resources. In situations like this, you have to be creative in determining how staff can be embedded in your library's community. Perhaps there is one staff member who will be the designated embedded librarian and can afford to devote time to various commitments, committees, activities, and plans. Or maybe that staff member has to choose whether he or she will be embedded in the business community relating to professionals, small business owners, or with job seekers, and then stay connected in a less-committed way with the other areas. Additionally, the embedded business librarian model can be divided among staff members who can determine where they are best suited in the business community. Whichever format you determine, there is no wrong answer. In our discussion about the difference between being embedded and providing outreach, we acknowledged that while being embedded can bring your relationships to the next level, outreach is a valuable asset to the library's community connections. So feel empowered to use a combination of outreach and embedded librarianship if your library's size or resources cannot commit to a fully embedded librarian.

THE LIAISON ASPECT OF YOUR JOB

While only you can determine what is best situated for the library and the library's community, the role of liaison will inevitably emerge from your continued and consistent interactions with the business community. This is an excellent opportunity for the library to serve as an equal partner for sharing information and providing connections to many business owners, professionals, and organizations because it is a low-key way to build such connections.

By definition, a liaison is "a person who helps organizations or groups to work together and provide information to each other."[1] Being a liaison also gives you an opportunity to develop a communication tool with the people and businesses that you connect with. As the liaison, you are serving as a connector of information, and this is important to your role and to your community.

Additionally, this is an optimal avenue for business owners or organizations that simply do not have the time to partner with you or collaborate with you in an embedded fashion. You can use this as a way to still stay connected and in the loop in the business community, while sharing resources and information with others as a liaison. The liaison role is a valuable way to leverage any limitations of embedded business librarianship.

This is important because it shows that the library is relevant to the needs and events in the area. But perhaps the most valuable aspect of being a liaison within the embedded role is that it keeps you current so that you can determine what are the evolving and emerging trends and opportunities faced by businesspeople, and continue to adjust your role as embedded librarian.

REFERRALS AND RECOMMENDATIONS

Whichever model of embedded business librarianship you have decided to implement, you will learn of new resources and make new connections with organizations, community colleges, business associations, and networking groups. In your relationships with small business owners, professionals, and job seekers, you will undoubtedly receive information about upcoming events, workshops, seminars, and opportunities that can benefit them. In a sense, you are becoming an information hub for business events and occurrences. This aspect of your role will include being a liaison among organizations, schools, committees, and businesses and to the community that you serve.

While you continue to foster relationships through your regular and consistent interactions, you will probably be asked to refer businesspeople's services to others in the community. Perhaps it is an attorney, realtor, broker, hair stylist, or restaurateur who would like you to promote their services within the library and also within your organizations. In situations such as this, it is important to remain

Suggestions for Handling Referrals

A strategy that is effective while not causing offense is stating: "Thank you so much for thinking of me. However, as a representative of the library, I focus on equally working with and for all (businesses/entrepreneurs/speakers/promoters) and don't promote one over the other." If you know of places in the area where they can freely promote their services, provide them with a list of these places.

Another way to address this issue is to set up workshops that teach the business community how to market their services themselves through social media. Hosting a "business blitz" class where you can teach them how to use Twitter, Instagram, Facebook, Pinterest, and more so that they can get their message out there, as well as hosting their own podcast series or video series with any circulating library equipment, is another great alternative. This way you can demonstrate that you care about the productivity and success of their businesses, but you are not going to promote one business over the other. Meanwhile you are still giving them the tools and the avenues to do it themselves. Consider partnering with another impartial organization like SCORE that can teach a class on how businesspeople can market their businesses, build up their electronic e-mail lists, or generate sales.

impartial and be clear that you do not promote businesses, products, or services. Admittedly, this can be difficult, especially as you grow to form unique relationships, and possibly genuinely believe in and care for the people that you are embedded with. It can be hard to not give preferential treatment either consciously or unconsciously while networking. But as a library professional, your duty is to serve the business community impartially and without bias. As you develop and deepen relationships, you want to demonstrate appreciation, while also making it clear that you are their partner and not their promoter.

SHARING INFORMATION

Throughout your role as an embedded librarian, you will also become a liaison *within* the connections that you form. As we discussed, you cannot promote businesses or people in the area. You can, however, share valuable resources and information that are free and beneficial to all businesspeople. Developing a tool that will allow you to spread information among members of the business community may help you become one of the central information points for business-area workshops, trainings, and informational sessions.

The tool that you use to share this information may be in the form of a blog, a designated discussion list for e-news, a community calendar that includes a specific segment for business-related functions and activities, or through social media, such as a Twitter or Facebook account for your role as a business librarian. You can make this tool a combination of services provided at the library, upcoming workshops that you are hosting, speaking engagements that you are conducting, and links to library resources, as well as training and workshops and informational sessions in the community.

The following are some examples of resources that you can share:

- Free online webinars and workshops provided by local organizations or businesses
- Networking events
- Job-seeker series

- Career center activities
- Village announcements for events like Small Business Saturday or promoting your small business through community-wide events

In whichever tool you decide to share information, whether it is a blog, community calendar, weekly e-blast, and so on, I would make a few suggestions:

- Keep the blog or other tool lively with a variety of media—not just blog posts, but incorporating videos, podcasts, community events, library programs, and informational interviews with local community members and business owners.
- Use the tool as a way to market the library's events, services, and resources.
- Use the tool as a way to get feedback from followers on the type of information that they want to the library to provide.
- Use the tool as an opportunity to bridge the gap between the businesses and people that you simply cannot partner with in any other way. This may be due to limited staff time, schedule, commitments, or other reasons. This is the ultimate way to still demonstrate that you care about businesspeople's success and about collaborating together in some form without a major commitment.

FILLING IN THE GAPS

The purpose of the liaison role is to ensure proper communication between the library and its patrons and the business community and its organizations.

In a sense, this aspect of the job can fill in those gaps where you want to have meaningful relationships with certain organizations or businesses, but cannot do so based on staff time, commitments, or focus as an embedded librarian. In this case, you can still maintain communication and a partnership-like connection with other organizations or businesses without the type of dedication that is required of a full-time embedded librarian. As a liaison, you are the person who is serving as a connector between resources and opportunities. You may develop a communication strictly based on monthly e-mails that update you on free workshops and trainings that you can pass along to patrons. This is the liaison role because you are not actively working with or partnering with the organization, but you are sharing valuable information with those who may need it.

As we discussed, not all aspects of your job can warrant being embedded or even engaged in active outreach, so in this instance being a liaison is especially useful and valuable. For example, if a job-seeker organization wants to partner with your library but it simply does not fit in your schedule and it is not possible to collaborate in any other way, an alternative could be to share their biweekly free Lunch and Learn sessions on your library's business blog. Something as simple as this can preserve relationships and ties in the business community by demonstrating that you do care about their progress. Many people are honored that you are willing to collaborate and are grateful that you maintain this blog because it introduces them to resources, events, and opportunities whose existence they would not have otherwise known about. This is a true form of serving as a liaison within the embedded librarian role.

FINAL THOUGHTS

In this chapter, we discussed being embedded and how that can take different forms depending on your library's staff size, talents, and the business community's needs. Specifically, we discussed the difference between being a liaison and an embedded business librarian. In essence, being a liaison means that you are committed to sharing valuable resources, information, and tools with your library's community and serving as a point of reference between various people and organizations. This helps bridge the gap between those areas of being embedded where you cannot be fully committed and dedicated and likewise with organizations and businesses that do not necessarily want to collaborate with you in an embedded manner. This is an example of how you can work together and demonstrate consideration and respect for an organization and business without partnering together otherwise. Sometimes it is little gestures like this that can serve you well down the road—always try to maintain some form of communication with anyone who reaches out to the library.

Additionally, we talked about what to do when serving as a liaison becomes tricky. Being a liaison is an inevitable role of being embedded; it naturally emerges as people come to you and want you to promote their services or products. It is important to be a liaison in a responsible and impartial manner rather than a liaison who functions in a manner that is inconsistent with the library's mission to serve as an equal access point for all forms of information and all patrons.

Lastly, the liaison role serves you well for solidifying your duty as a respected figure in the library's business community. As librarians, we connect people to information in the form of tools, resources, and databases on a regular basis. But it is also crucial when we can connect them to services, workshops, networking events, and seminars that are local because these can perhaps introduce them to people who can have a direct impact on their life, business, career search, and more; that is perhaps the most important aspect of being a liaison within the embedded role. Yes, it is possible to be embedded without being a liaison, and it is possible to be a liaison without being embedded, but when you combine the two aspects, it creates a synergy that ensures that you and your library are part of the conversation in the business community.

LET'S SUM IT UP

- Depending on your library's staff and size, you may have to incorporate embedded business librarian aspects within different roles or initiatives. Start small and make adjustments as you go along the way.
- Through the liaison role, we are able to maintain communications with a variety of people, stay current on local events, and share information with the community in a way that keeps us as part of the ongoing conversation.
- Develop policies and procedures to handle situations where members of the business community would like to use the library as an opportunity to gain clients through programming, referrals, or other methods.
- The liaison role reminds us that while we cannot be all things to everyone, we can maintain communication in small but significant ways with members of the business community.

NOTE

1. Merriam-Webster, March 16, 2016, www.merriamwebster.com/dictionary/liaison.

7
Continuing Education for the Embedded Business Librarian

IN THIS CHAPTER, WE WILL LEARN

- Recommended books, websites, videos, podcasts, blogs, courses, and news sources for continuing education

- How to join or start a networking group for fellow library professionals

By now you have done thorough research on your library's business community, developed a strategy for building community connections, and created platforms that you can use for library programs and initiatives. This is quite an accomplishment, so give yourself a round of applause. Surely throughout this process you have also learned about new ways that you can expand your expertise as an embedded business librarian, as well as how the library can be more adaptable to the needs of the community.

In this chapter, we are going to talk about the importance of continuing your education within this role. Depending on your professional and educational background, you may already have business knowledge or you may simply be in this position because your manager appointed you to it. Regardless of your past experiences, in moving forward as an embedded business librarian, you will need to stay abreast in your knowledge of business resources and information. This will help you stay focused on what is current and trending in the business community. Let's review the ways that you can continue your education as an embedded business librarian.

Keep the purpose of your role as an embedded business librarian at the forefront of your decisions, particularly when you feel overwhelmed, intimidated, or self-conscious. When you remind yourself of what your duties do and do not entail, you can put yourself at ease and lessen the pressure that you may be putting on yourself to "know it all."

Nevertheless, you will need to be knowledgeable about business terminology, resources, and statistics so that you can professionally and confidently direct your business community to the appropriate information. Additionally, having business knowledge will improve your intellectual and emotional understanding of the situations and issues that business owners, professionals, and job seekers face. Above all, you will feel more confident when you are teaching, instructing, and explaining business resources and lessons to your community.

BOOKS

As the embedded business librarian, you may be the one to select the business books for your library's collection and provide monthly reviews and recommendations of these books to the business blog, social media, local Chamber of Commerce, or other outlet. Not only does this promote the library collection, and help you get to know the collection on a deeper level, but it also exposes you to current and emerging business trends and techniques that enhance your knowledge of this field.

The thought of reading business books may sound extremely dull. Maybe you conjure images of books analyzing the stock market

Q & A

I don't have a business degree or business background. Can I fill the role of an embedded business librarian?

There are some business librarians who will be in this role with prior business experience, whether that was owning a business, studying business, or prior professional work in the business sector. Librarians with this prior background will undoubtedly be equipped with extensive knowledge and experiences that will help them relate to their library's business community.

But for many librarians, this will be brand-new territory. Because of the evolving needs of our communities and libraries, you may be a librarian who was appointed to this position because of your adaptability and your dedication to customer service. Your library clearly felt that you were a good fit for this role based on your skills and talents. Being an embedded business librarian keeps your role interesting, challenging, and exciting. Furthermore, you learn more about yourself since you must leave your comfort zone and expand your expertise.

Regardless, some people shy away from this role or lack the confidence to go out into the community and make their presence known because they feel that without the appropriate academic or professional background, they are inept at helping the business community.

Let's be clear: this is incorrect. Although you may not have the business background that is a great aid to the librarians who do possess it, you can nonetheless be an important asset to your community. As librarians, it is our duty to direct our community to the resources and information that will add value to their lives. In previous chapters, we talked about the differentiation between being an embedded business librarian and being a business coach or career advisor. It is not your responsibility to give advice on career paths or business plans. You are directing professionals, business owners, and job seekers to the information and tools that will empower them to make their own informed decisions and choices.

or developing a business plan. Well, yes, business books can be these things, but they can also be more about business development concepts and philosophies. If you decide to form a business book discussion group at your library or in partnership with a business organization, these books can prove to be quite valuable. The following is a list of recommended books:

Making Sense of Business Reference: A Guide for Librarians and Research Professionals, by Celia Ross (ALA Editions, 2013)

Talk Like Ted: The 9 Public-Speaking Secrets of the World's Top Minds, by Carmine Gallo (St. Martin's Press, 2014)

Lean In: Women, Work, and the Will to Succeed, by Sheryl Sandberg (Knopf, 2013)

Without Their Permission: How the 21st Century Will Be Made, Not Managed, by Alexis Ohanian (Business Plus, October 2013)

The Lean Startup: How Today's Entrepreneurs Use Continuous Innovation to Create Radically Successful Businesses, by Eric Ries (Crown Business, 2011)

Leaders Eat Last: Why Some Teams Pull Together and Others Don't, by Simon Sinek (Portfolio, 2014)

Start with Why: How Great Leaders Inspire Everyone to Take Action, by Simon Sinek (Portfolio, 2011)

Delivering Happiness: A Path to Profits, Passion, and Purpose, by Tony Hsieh (Grand Central Publishing, 2010)

The Artist's Way at Work, by Mark Bryan, Julia Cameron, and Catherine Allen (William Morrow Paperbacks, 1998)

The Tipping Point: How Little Things Can Make a Big Difference, by Malcolm Gladwell (Little, Brown, 2000)

The Rise of the Creative Class: And How It's Transforming Work, Leisure, Community, and Everyday Life, by Richard Florida (Basic Books, 2002)

Presence: Bringing Your Boldest Self to Your Biggest Challenges, by Amy Cuddy (Little, Brown, 2015)

While many of the books listed above can be beneficial to business owners, professionals, and job seekers alike, the following books are specifically for those in career transitions:

Coach Yourself to a New Career: 7 Steps to Reinventing Your Professional Life, by Talane Miedaner (McGraw-Hill Education, 2010)

Career Distinction: Stand Out by Building Your Brand, by William Arruda (Wiley, 2007)

The Defining Decade: Why Your Twenties Matter and How to Make the Most of Them Now, by Meg Jay (Twelve, 2012)

Life Reimagined: Discovering Your New Life Opportunities, by Richard Leider (Berrett-Koehler, 2013)

The 20-Minute Networking Meeting: How Little Meetings Can Lead to Your Next Big Job, by Marcia Ballinger (Keystone Search, 2012)

WEBSITES

Peruse the websites of your community's businesses, organizations, and career centers. Subscribing to the e-news of as many local business owners, companies, organizations, and career centers as possible, as well as the Chamber of Commerce and your town or village, will help you stay informed about local events, updates, and news so you can determine ways the library can collaborate, as well as direct patrons to relevant local resources and tools.

Additionally, below is a list of websites for regular reading and subscribing to their e-newsletters. They will help boost your knowledge of business and job-seeker strategies, as well as keep you in the loop about trending topics and issues on a national and global level.

- The Daily Muse, www.themuse.com/advice

  Career advice, job search resources, and helpful tools and technologies

- Mashable, http://mashable.com

  Content for small businesses, job seekers, marketing, advertising, and technology

- Social Media Examiner, www.socialmediaexaminer.com

  Social media marketing tools and techniques to share with small business owners

- Investopedia, www.investopedia.com

  Tutorials, personal finance, wealth management, and dictionary for business terminology

- DailyWorth, www.dailyworth.com

  Career information, freelancing, running a business, and financial resources for women

- Inc., www.inc.com

  Special business reports, investing, innovation, and startup information

- Entrepreneur, www.entrepreneur.com

  Various business models and resources, growth strategies, leadership, and technology

- Fast Company, www.fastcompany.com

  Career, creation, balancing professional and personal life tools

VIDEOS AND PODCASTS

Sometimes the best way to learn about business resources, terminology, and tools is visually or by listening. Below is a list of videos and podcasts to keep you informed about business and careers.

- Fast Company's 30 Second MBA, http://bit.ly/20D1gp6

  Less than one-minute videos by leading business and leadership experts

- TedTalks, http://bit.ly/1qkgCMD

  Listen to innovative and inspiring topics on podcast or watch on YouTube or in an app

- Entrepreneur On Fire, www.eofire.com

  Podcast with important conversations from various visionaries and business luminaries

- Smart Passive Income, http://bit.ly/1edTWus

  Podcasts for entrepreneurs to create digital products and sell online

- The $100 MBA Show, http://apple.co/20YqfZy

  Ten-minute podcasts on key business strategies and tips to implement

COURSES

Take business, career, and leadership courses for free online or share them with your business community. These structured courses will help you stay organized and motivated as you continue to learn new concepts. The following is a list of online courses:

- Coursera, www.coursera.org

  Free courses taught from universities around the world. Courses have included job search strategies, building career confidence, basic business concepts, entrepreneurship, and new global economies.

- EdX, www.edx.org

  Free courses with topics including business management, corporate social responsibility, startup success, resume, networking, and interview skills

- Harvard Open Learning Initiative, http://bit.ly/1mGxkLx

  Business management, computer science, economics, and finance

- Khan Academy, www.khanacademy.org

  Economics and finance courses explained simply and clearly

- Morningstar Investing Classroom, www.morningstar .com/cover/Classroom.html

  Detailed tutorials on stocks, funds, bonds, and portfolio with regular webinars

- Business 101: Introduction to Business, https://learn .saylor.org/course/bus101

  Introductory course that gives an overview of business from context to marketing and banking

- Business Reference 101 with Celia Ross, www.ala.org/ rusa/development/businessreference101

  Celia Ross goes over important business resources and research strategies in this four-week class

BUSINESS NEWS SOURCES

Stay up-to-date on business news and how it will impact the small business owners, professionals, and job seekers in your community. Creating Google News alerts, as well as setting up a Twitter list for business-related news sources, are easy options. Additionally, if your library has print or digital copies of these news sources, you can scan them regularly. Here are some recommended news sources:

- Business Insider, www.businessinsider.com
- TechCrunch, http://techcrunch.com
- *New York Times*, www.nytimes.com
- *The Economist*, www.economist.com
- Reuters, www.reuters.com
- Bloomberg Business, www.bloomberg.com
- *Wall Street Journal*, www.wsj.com

BLOGS

Lastly, blogs can be an excellent way to stay in the know, as well as get personal insights into the business landscape.

- LinkedIn Today (Pulse), https://www.linkedin.com/pulse
  Receive updates about posts created by your LinkedIn connections, as well as other industry experts
- Duct Tape Marketing Blog, www.ducttapemarketing .com/blog
  Information for marketing consultants, coaches, small business owners, and entrepreneurs

NETWORKING WITH LIBRARY PROFESSIONALS

The above resources can be absolutely invaluable to you in staying current in business information and trends. However, it is just as important to stay connected with fellow librarians who also work with their business communities. When you are part of a group that connects regularly, you can share ideas, get inspired, receive support and encouragement, and learn from one another. The connections that you build within the library community are just as important as the connections you build in your library's business community. Here are three easy and sustainable ways to get involved:

The easiest and least time-intensive is to simply join a business librarians' discussion list. Business librarians throughout the country ask one another reference and outreach questions, share information about upcoming grants, awards, and programs, and discuss important committee activities and conferences. The BUSLIB-L discussion list is a popular choice that describes itself as "an electronic forum that addresses all issues relating to: the collection, storage, dissemination of Business Information within a library setting." Go to https://sites.google.com/site/buslibl/.

If you have more time in your schedule, consider joining an American Library Association (ALA) committee or participating in the ALA's webinars, initiatives, and conference events. The ALA's Business Reference in Public Libraries Committee meets to "study, promote, and support the role of business reference in public libraries." Go to http://bit.ly/1QlMnBV.

Find or form a local business interest group in your area. If there are other business librarians or embedded/outreach librarians nearby, try forming a group that connects quarterly. I recommend contacting your state library or state's library association and asking if there are any interest groups in your area. If you do not find any interest groups and librarians are limited on time, consider using free virtual networking tools like Google Hangouts to meet and collaborate. Go to https://hangouts.google.com/.

FINAL THOUGHTS

In this chapter, we discussed the importance of staying current in business resources, news, and trends. This may seem like a lot of information to digest, but if you develop an action plan, this can be sustainable and fun. When you are constantly and consistently learning, self-educating, and expanding your knowledge of this area, you will be inspired to create new initiatives for your library and business community, as well as understand the path of the business owners, professionals, and job seekers in a more meaningful way. Take a look at the books, videos/podcasts, websites, courses, news sites, and blogs listed in this chapter to determine what you would reasonably and energetically like to accomplish on a daily, weekly, and monthly basis.

Additionally, we discussed the importance of collaborating with fellow librarians. This can be accomplished by joining electronic discussion lists, committees, and interest groups. Only you can decide what is the most manageable for your schedule, but realize that when you build those relationships with your library colleagues, you open the door for inspiration and new opportunities.

LET'S SUM IT UP

- There are a variety of ways to keep learning. From reading business books to subscribing to news sources to taking online courses and training, create a continuing education plan that keeps you motivated and willing to learn.
- Developing a network with fellow library professionals can help you overcome fear, share ideas, and create a supportive environment.
- The key takeaway from this chapter is to stay connected, informed, and always learning.

8

Putting It All Together

IN THIS CHAPTER, WE WILL LEARN

- How to combine all of the different aspects of the embedded business librarianship role

- Quick and easy ways to get going when you don't know how to move forward

- The importance of getting to work

Well, we've had quite a journey on the path to embedded business librarianship. It may feel like a whirlwind, so this is the perfect opportunity to summarize everything that we've discussed. By the end of this chapter, you'll feel empowered to take on all of the challenges and endeavors that this role encompasses. We will even have some suggestions for getting started when you feel stuck before concluding our time together with some final words of inspiration and encouragement.

CHAPTER EIGHT

ALL THE PIECES OF THE PUZZLE

We started this book by discussing the core concepts of embedded business librarianship, its goals, and how it differs from outreach. By now, you have a solid foundation of the principles and practices of embedded business librarianship as it relates to the library and the community. Unlike outreach where the primary objective is to promote the library's resources and refocus attention on the library, embedded business librarianship seeks to build relationships that go beyond transactional ones to interactional ones. This means that you will ultimately be interspersed in the business community through ongoing partnerships, committee work, and open and honest dialogue with local business owners, professionals, and job seekers. Additionally, being embedded in the business community will involve constant and consistent engagement on a meaningful level with the ultimate goal of being viewed as an equal partner.

The path to embedded business librarianship begins with some background research. We discussed the importance of getting a better understanding of the economic and industry situation of your public library's community. The information gathered is not necessarily to assume or predict where the library can fill voids, but rather to bolster yourself with the details, concepts, and trends that impact the members of your library's business community. Having this knowledge will certainly help you prepare for more purposeful conversations and make connections with opportunities in the community and library. Additionally, reaching out to one or two members of the business community for an informal informational interview can help guide you in the right direction as you start to prepare for stepping outside the library.

Moving along, the next step is to actually start putting yourself out into the community and becoming embedded. The best way to do this is to develop an action plan for making initial connections and building upon the relationships that you form. Initially you will gather a list of contacts that you can reach out to and then set up a meeting. At the meeting, your objective will be to inform them more about yourself, the library, and your interest in the business community. You will also use this opportunity to learn more about their background and their aspirations. Afterward, it is best to create a call to action where you can continue to connect with them through an event at the library, training session, or other opportunity. Your focus will then be to continue to network in the community and build connections. It is important to remember that these steps outlined are not the practice of being embedded; rather it is the steps that are needed to *become* embedded in the business community.

When interacting with business owners, professionals, and job seekers, it is necessary to approach each group as unique and distinct from the others. This means that your interactions will be varied, as well as the type of ongoing relationships that you have with them. It is important to understand what you are able to reasonably provide as the embedded business librarian and where it is necessary to refer them to other resources or organizations. Additionally, you will develop sustainable pathways for maintaining consistent communication with each unique group of the business community.

Once you have evolved in your role as the embedded business librarian, you can start to implement in the library some of the feedback that you learn from business owners, professionals, and job seekers. This means adjusting services, programs, initiatives, and workshops. There are plenty of tutorials and trainings that you can provide, but it is necessary to understand when you should employ professionals, as well as unbiased organizations that can provide meaningful financial, legal, or health-related workshops. Furthermore, equip yourself with practices and procedures for handling local business owners who may view the library as an opportunity to market their services or products. Perhaps the most unique opportunities for engagement in the library are through networking events and coworking spaces. There are a variety of networking events that your library can implement, and creating a coworking environment can encourage interaction with entrepreneurs, as well as professionals and job seekers. The relationships that you form in the business community will drive these new implementations in the library.

As you develop and shape this role for your library and the business community's needs, you may need to make adjustments to make it flexible and sustainable. For some libraries, this could mean sharing the responsibilities of embedded business librarianship among staff or being embedded in only one aspect of your business community. Whichever model you employ in your library is a mark of success, provided that the focal point of developing and deepening relationships in the business community is upheld. Additionally, the liaison aspect of being embedded can help fill in the gaps where you are unable to give your full attention. As a liaison, you can develop a regular blog, social media account, calendar, e-newsletter, or some other tool that keeps the business community engaged and active with one another and the library. This can be an excellent alternative to share with members of the business community when you are unable to be embedded in certain areas.

Throughout your role as the embedded business librarian, continue your education through books, blogs, news sources, podcasts, video tutorials, online courses, and more. This is an evolving field and role and the more that you continually learn, the more confident you will feel and the more creative opportunities you will see develop in your role. Do not feel that a business degree is required; instead, challenge yourself to develop your craft and expertise in regard to business topics. Lastly, build relationships with fellow library professionals locally, regionally, and nationally to get inspired, share advice, and learn from one another.

SO, WHAT'S NEXT?

Sometimes the number of options or future plans can feel paralyzing. You may feel a combination of excitement and uncertainty about getting started. If you are feeling stuck and don't know how to proceed, here are some quick and easy tips for getting inspired without leaving your desk. Refer back to these suggestions whenever you need to get recharged:

> List a handful of the businesses, organizations, and career centers that you would like to develop relationships with

and start following them on social media or subscribing to their blogs or discussion lists. This will help you start learning more about them, as well as make you aware of upcoming opportunities to connect with them.

Watch a TED Talk (www.ted.com/talks) or head over to The Daily Muse (www.themuse.com/advice) to learn some interesting new facts or resources about business, technology, leadership, careers, and networking. Consider how these can impact your role and interactions with the business community.

Look at any community calendars that list upcoming events, open houses, job fairs, or ribbon cuttings. Can't find any? Look on Meetup.com to see if there are upcoming local entrepreneur, business, or job-seeker events. Commit yourself to attending one that interests you.

Develop or create a business- or career-related tutorial about a library resource that you can upload to the library's YouTube or Slideshare account and post it on social media to boost your confidence in this topic and get your voice heard.

Do some basic research about local business sizes or industry trends on a national scale. Get informed about what is going on both locally and nationally and consider how this can impact your business community, as well as your role as an embedded business librarian.

JUST GET STARTED

You have everything that you need to start building transformative relationships in your library's business community. And don't worry, you don't need to have everything perfectly mapped out to get the ball rolling. Like many other librarian roles, this will involve a great deal of strategic planning, innovation, and making changes along the way. The model that you are implementing today will transform and evolve into something completely new in the coming months as you start to become more aware of your business community. But the most important thing is that you must get started. Without getting into action, you will never know where you can make adjustments and improvements.

Clarity comes through action. You can plan and strategize for months, but the most powerful messages you will receive and the ideas you will have will be a direct result of taking action. This is precisely why the background research aspect of this job is minimal: you will learn more from actually speaking with the business community members and starting to develop connections with them.

At times you may wonder if your role is making a difference or an impact on the community, and other times you will be overwhelmed with the new relationships that you form. Understand that your duties as an embedded business librarian are atypical and you are undoubtedly treading on new territory for yourself and your library and community.

Will there be trial and errors? Absolutely. Will you make U-turns on certain decisions or actions? Most likely. But you can't make progress without putting one step forward. So don't be afraid to start small. Don't belittle yourself for easing your way into this role. Be patient as you insert yourself into the community in a brand-new way.

FINAL THOUGHTS

You should feel confident that you have all of the tools and steps that you need to make this role unique and particular to your library and your community. Continue learning, growing, exploring, evolving, and adapting in this role and how it relates to the business owners, professionals, and job seekers in your area. But, most importantly, be proud of yourself and the progress that you are making for your library and the business community that you serve. You are more than prepared to start building transformative relationships in your library's business community as the embedded business librarian.

Bibliography

Brooks, Chad. "'Solopreneurs' Redefining Work." *Business News Daily*. October 7, 2014. www.businessnewsdaily.com/7246 -freelance-workers-solopreneurs.html.

Distel, Shannon, and Julie Kittredge. Interview with Barbara Alvarez. Arlington Heights, IL, March 2, 2016.

"Frequently Asked Questions about Small Business." U.S. Small Business Administration, SBA.gov. March 2014. www.sba.gov/ advocacy/frequently-asked-questions-about-small-business.

Horrigan, John B. "Libraries at the Crossroads." Pew Research Center Internet Science Tech RSS. September 15, 2015. www .pewinternet.org/2015/09/15/libraries-at-the-crossroads/.

MBO Partners, "State of Independence in America 2015." September 1, 2013. https://www.mbopartners.com/state-of-independence.

Merriam-Webster, s.v. "liaison." www.merriamwebster.com/ dictionary/liaison.

Palmer, Kent. Interview with Barbara Alvarez. Naperville, IL, March 2, 2016.

"Public Library Funding & Technology Access Study 2011–2012." American Library Association. www.ala.org/research/plftas/2011_2012.

"Small Business Trends." U.S. Small Business Administration, SBA.gov. https://www.sba.gov/content/small-business-trends-impact.

Spors, Kelly K. "Is a Small-Business Owner Always an Entrepreneur?" WSJ, *Wall Street Journal*. September 16, 2008. www.wsj.com/articles/SB122153790674841873.

Taylor, Kate. "The Difference between a Solopreneur and a Side-Gigger (Infographic)." Entrepreneur. November 9, 2014. www.entrepreneur.com/article/239522.

Thompson, Derek. "A World without Work." *Atlantic* 316, no. 1 (July 2015): 50–61.

Zickuhr, Kathryn, Lee Rainie, Kristen Purcell, and Maeve Duggan. "How Americans Value Public Libraries in Their Communities." Pew Internet Libraries RSS. Pew Research Center. December 11, 2013. http://libraries.pewinternet.org/2013/12/11/libraries-in-communities.

Index

CPSIA information can be obtained
at www.ICGtesting.com
Printed in the USA
LVOW04s0034070117

520028LV00013B/283/P

9 780838 914748